# GOD'S COVENANT OF HEALING

by

S.J. HILL

ENJOYING GOD MINISTRIES

S. J. Hill
P. O. Box 918
Grandview, MO 64030
www.sjhill.com

ISBN 0-9673378-1-X

All scriptures are taken from the New King James Version copyright 1982 by Thomas Nelson, Inc. unless indicated otherwise.

Book cover design by
David Ervin at Firefly Studios
www.fireflystudios.net

Book layout and production by
George Payne at Write Hand Publishing
www.writehand.com

# Table of Contents

Is it the will of God to heal His people of their sicknesses and pains? This chapter deals with the foundational truths of healing and establishes the fact that God has entered into a covenant of healing with His people through the finished work of the Cross.

Why did Job have boils? Are some people sick for the glory of God? Is healing really provided through the Atonement of Christ, or was Matthew 8:17 fulfilled during His earthly ministry? What about Paul's thorn and the sicknesses of Trophimus and Epaphroditus? This chapter contains a thorough study of God's Word concerning these and other vital questions regarding the subject of healing.

One of the first principles in treating any illness is discovering and, in turn, eliminating the cause of the sickness. Through insight from the Word of God, this chapter may help you find the reasons why you haven't been healed, enabling you to remove the obstacles which may have prevented you from experiencing healing.

Once the obstacles and hindrances to your faith have been removed, you will be in a much better position to receive your healing. It's important that you act on the principles mentioned within this chapter in order for you to experience the fulfillment of God's promise of healing in your life.

The Bible is not only clear in its teaching on how to receive healing but also on how to keep the healing once it's experienced. As you apply the principles in this chapter, you'll be able to stand against any counterattack of the enemy who, at times, will try to rob you of your healing.

# Introduction

**O**ver the years, many people have been healed by the power of God as a result of prayer and the teaching they have received on the subject of healing. Yet, far too many individuals are still sick and in desperate need of a miracle.

During my travels, I've discovered the need for a practical and concise book on healing which can be read and understood by the average person–a book that's not only inspirational but also deals with the questions and problems encountered by those seeking healing. It's with this purpose in mind that I've written on the subject of *God's Covenant of Healing*. I believe this book will quicken faith in the lives of those who have had little or no previous knowledge of the subject of divine healing, as well as restore faith to individuals who have sought, yet failed, to receive healing.

It's my prayer that through reading this book many will learn to not only appropriate the benefits of the Cross which are promised in the Word of God but live a life of faith and walk in the reality of healing and health.

S. J.

# CHAPTER I

# Redeemed From Disease

**O**ne of the greatest hindrances to receiving healing is a lack of understanding that it is the will of God to heal His people. Until we know His will, there's nothing upon which to base our faith, because faith's foundation is the Word of God. We have to know what the Father has promised so that all doubt can be removed and a strong faith developed. There can be no uncertainty and apprehension about His will if we're going to exercise faith for healing.

A person who needs healing, but doesn't know that it's God's will to heal him, is like a farmer trying to reap a harvest without first planting seed. It's the living Word planted as seed within the heart of an individual that will heal his physical body. Psalm 107:20 states that God

> *...sent His word and healed them, And delivered them from their destructions.*

Complete deliverance from sickness will only come from comprehending what God has revealed in His Word. Jesus said, "And you shall know the truth, and the truth shall make you free" (John 8:32).

If possible, before requesting prayer for healing, a person

should first receive sufficient instruction regarding the truths of healing, because faith for healing comes just as it does for all the promises of God–by hearing and obeying the Word of God (Romans 10:17). There's absolutely no substitute for God's Word, not even prayer!

It's of the utmost importance for us to see that a lack of instruction will always result in a lack of faith. For example, Jesus couldn't do any significant miracles in Nazareth, except He laid hands on a few sick people and healed them. And the Bible says Jesus "...marveled because of their unbelief" (Mark 6:5-6). No doubt, one of the reasons for their unbelief was their need of instruction. Jesus, in seeing this, "...went about the villages in a circuit, teaching" (Mark 6:6).

Over the years, I've dealt with a number of people who have had outstanding men and women of God pray for them to be healed. Even so, some of these same individuals have reported they were not healed and are still suffering physically. This has been due, in part, to the idea that all that was necessary for them to experience their healing was for some prominent person to lay hands on them and pray for them. However, healing is a matter of personal faith in Christ and His unchangeable Word. What these people actually needed was instruction from the Word of God, as well as prayer for their healing. Proverbs 4:13 says, "Take firm hold of instruction, do not let her go; Keep her; for she is your life."

Many people are wasting away with sickness and struggling in faith because they haven't had the opportunity to be taught from the Word of God, or they've failed to heed the instruction when it was given. As you study the principles found within this book, I pray you will respond in faith and obedience and experience real freedom from your physical problems.

## Sickness Began with the Fall

In considering the matter of healing, we have to begin with the very first chapter of the Book of Genesis. After God had finished His six days of creative work, we read, "Then God saw everything that He had made, and indeed it was very good..." (Genesis 1:31).

God had made man in His own image, having breathed into man's nostrils the breath of life. He had surrounded the first couple with unspeakable beauty and splendor. What an experience it must've been for Adam to have enjoyed the incomparable fragrance of a newly made world! He knew no heartache, no sorrow, and no distress. He felt no weakness of any kind. Sickness and pain were completely unknown in the Garden of Eden. All that God had made in His infinite wisdom, power, and love was perfect in every way.

It wasn't until sin entered into the world that sickness first made its appearance in various forms. Man's rebellion not only produced untold suffering and distress but also paved the way for disease, decay, and even death. Had there been no sin, there wouldn't have been any sickness or pain. It's imperative for us to see that sickness not only came **after** man sinned but also as a **result** of sin.

## Sickness–A Result of Sin

Throughout the Old Testament we find examples of individuals who were afflicted with sickness as a consequence of their sin and disobedience toward God (Numbers 12:1-15; 21:1-9). This truth is reinforced in Deuteronomy 28 where we read of the results for breaking covenant with God:

> *But it shall come to pass, if you do not obey the voice of the LORD your God, to observe carefully all His commandments and His statutes which I command*

*you today, that all these curses will come upon you, and overtake you: Cursed shall you be in the city, and cursed shall you be in the country. Cursed shall be your basket and your kneading bowl. Cursed shall be the fruit of your body, and the produce of your land, the increase of your cattle and the offspring of your flocks. Cursed shall you be when you come in, and cursed shall you be when you go out. The LORD will send on you cursing, confusion, and rebuke in all that you set your hand to do, until you are destroyed and until you perish quickly, because of the wickedness of your doings in which you have forsaken Me. The LORD will make the plague cling to you until He has consumed you from the land you are going to possess. The LORD will strike you with consumption, with fever, with inflammation, with severe burning fever, with the sword, with scorching, and with mildew; they shall pursue you until you perish (vs. 15-22).*

The curse of the Law is further described in the same chapter, as follows:

*The LORD will strike you with the boils of Egypt, with tumors, with the scab, and with the itch, from which you cannot be healed. The LORD will strike you with madness and blindness and confusion of heart. And you shall grope at noon-day, as a blind man gropes in darkness; you shall not prosper in your ways; you shall be only oppressed and plundered continually, and no one shall save you....The LORD will strike you in the knees and on the legs with severe boils which cannot be healed, and from the sole of*

10

*your foot to the top of your head.... If you do not care-
fully observe all the words of this law that are written
in this book, that you may fear this glorious and awesome name, THE LORD YOUR GOD; then the LORD
will bring upon you and your descendants extraordinary plagues–great and prolonged plagues–and serious and prolonged sicknesses. Moreover He will bring
back on you all the diseases of Egypt, of which you
were afraid, and they shall cling to you. Also every
sickness, and every plague, which is not written in this
Book of the Law, will the LORD bring upon you until
you are destroyed (vs. 27-29, 35, 58-61).*

Even though only some sicknesses were specifically mentioned in this passage–blindness, botch [boils], consumption
[tuberculosis], emerods [tumors], extreme burning, fever, inflammation, itch, madness, scab [includes skin diseases]–according to
verse 61, every disease was to be seen as part of the curse for vio-
lating God's covenant.

Although it's implied in the text, we shouldn't assume that
God afflicts man with sickness and pain. While the Old Testament
in particular magnifies the absolute, sovereign control of God over
everything, when we study the full revelation of Scripture, it's
obvious that Satan is the one who tries to destroy the human race
with sickness. Even though it appears from verse 61 that God
would bring all kinds of terrible plagues upon His people if they
disobeyed Him, the Hebrew word for "bring" is to be used in the
**permissive** sense and not in the **causative** sense. A better way to
understand what I'm referring to is to read verse 61 as follows:

*Also every sickness and every plague, which is not
written in the Book of the Law, will the LORD allow*

11

*[permit] to be brought upon you, until you are destroyed.*

This same principle can also be applied to Exodus 15:26, where God said,

*...If you diligently heed the voice of the LORD your God and do that which is right in His sight, give ear to His commandments and keep all His statutes, I will put none of the diseases on you which I have brought on the Egyptians. For I am the LORD who heals you.*

Again, in using the "permissive sense" to translate this verse, it would read,

*...I will not **allow** any of these diseases to be put upon you, which I have **permitted** to be brought upon the Egyptians. For I am the LORD who heals you (emphasis added).*

When God's people willfully broke His covenant through **continual** sin and disobedience, they found themselves no longer under His divine protection, and as a result, various kinds of diseases were **allowed** to come upon them.

We can't picture sickness and pain in the Garden of Eden prior to the entrance of sin into the world. The Fall was the work of Satan; therefore, we can only conclude that sin and sickness must have the same origin.

## Sickness-the Work of Satan

Satan is the author of all sickness and disease as is clearly seen in several passages in the Word of God. The Book of Job, for example, unmistakably shows us that it was the devil who "...struck

Job with painful boils from the sole of his foot to the crown of his head" (Job 2:7).

According to Luke 13, Jesus went into the synagogue on the Sabbath and met

> ...*a woman who had a spirit of infirmity eighteen years, and was bent over and could in no way raise herself up. But when Jesus saw her, He called her to Him and said to her, "Woman, you are loosed from your infirmity." And he laid His hands on her, and immediately she was made straight, and glorified God (Luke 13:11-13).*

In the meantime, the ruler of the synagogue had become angry with Christ because He had healed this woman on the Sabbath. Yet Jesus replied,

> ...*ought not this woman, being a daughter of Abraham, whom Satan has bound–think of it–these eighteen years, be loosed from this bond on the Sabbath (v. 16)?*

Notice, Jesus declared that this woman had actually been afflicted by Satan! In John 10:10, the devil is depicted as an adversary who has come to kill, steal, and destroy. Preaching to the household of Cornelius, Peter said,

> ...*God anointed Jesus of Nazareth with the Holy Spirit and with power, who went about doing good, and healing all that were **oppressed** by the devil; for God was with him (Acts 10:38, emphasis added).*

Satan is not only the originator of sickness but he also has certain demonic spirits under his power, whose primary function is to make people sick. (See Mark 9:25 and Luke 4:39.) The fact that Jesus cured many people by casting out evil spirits proves He regarded disease to be of satanic origin.

From the beginning, it has been in the heart of God to heal His people and deliver them from the hands of their enemies. This is the reason Jesus' work of redemption included destroying the works [e.g., sickness] of the devil (1 John 3:8).

## God's Covenant of Healing

The earliest promise of healing can be found in Exodus 15:25-26. Having crossed the Red Sea, Moses led the children of Israel through the desert for three days without water. When they eventually found water, they discovered it was bitter and undrink-able. As Moses cried to the Lord for help, God showed him a tree, and when Moses cast it into the water, the water became sweet.

In this passage, the sweetening of the bitter waters of Marah was closely connected with the ordinance of healing which God immediately proceeded to give to Israel. It's evident that the healing of the water was intended to represent the promise of physical heal-ing made by the Lord.

We also need to notice how early this experience is found in the history of the nation of Israel. The promise of healing was given after God delivered His people from Egypt and at the very begin-ning of their journey toward the land of Canaan. It's significant that the first covenant promise God made with His people after the crossing of the Red Sea was the promise of healing.

It was also at this time that God revealed Himself to Israel as their Physician. Through the redemptive and covenant Name of Yahweh Roph'eka [which is translated as "The Lord who heals you" or "The Lord your Physician"], God pledged to meet all of Israel's physical needs as they loved and obeyed Him.

What's the relevance of all this to us?

First of all, the tree shown to Moses was symbolic of Jesus' death on the Cross which removed the bitter effects of sin [including sickness] placed upon mankind. Just as it was necessary for Moses to cast the tree which God had provided into the waters before they could be made sweet, even so, it's essential for us as believers to appropriate by faith the blessings the Lord has provided for us through the Cross. For anyone to be saved or healed, there must be personal faith in Christ as both Savior and Healer.

Secondly, Israel's journey out of Egypt and through the Red Sea is a type of our redemption and deliverance from sin and all its power. Just as God encouraged His people at the beginning of their pilgrimage with the promise of healing, it's still the desire of our heavenly Father to encourage us at the start of our Christian journey with the same promise. As we walk in faith and loving obedience, we can expect to be delivered from sin and sickness, both of which belong to the "old life of bondage" we left behind.

Thirdly, the covenant of healing found in Exodus 15:25-26 is much older than the Law given to Moses on Mt. Sinai and, therefore, hasn't been done away merely by the passing of the Law. Just as Paul told the Galatians that the covenant of Abraham couldn't be annulled by the later Law of Moses, even so, the covenant promise of healing must stand after the passing away of all the Mosaic institutions. The very terms "statute" and "ordinance" speak of the permanency of this divine promise given to all the people of God.

Finally, in revealing Himself as Yahweh Roph'eka ["The Lord who heals you"], God was forever expressing His purpose, as well as His character, to His people. All that He would make known of Himself through His redemptive names under the older covenant would later be fulfilled in Jesus. James 1:17 declares that with God there is "...no variableness, neither shadow of turning." This simply means He doesn't change, even slightly. If God was Yahweh Roph'eka under the older, inferior covenant, it's impossible to view Christ as Someone other than our Healer under the new and better covenant.

## Healing–the Work of Christ

The Gospels record twenty-six cases of individual healings accomplished under the ministry of Jesus Christ. In ten instances, the healing of the sick is mentioned without stating the nature of the diseases that were cured. On four occasions, it's said that Christ went from place to place healing everyone that came to Him (Matthew 4:23-24; 8:16-17; 12:15; 14:35-36).

All of these testimonies graphically show that Christ's ministry of healing was not merely an occasional, unimportant feature of His work of redemption. In the life and work of the Son of God, healing the sick played a primary role!

Jesus didn't seem to have any apprehension whatsoever that His miracles of healing might distract from what was essential–the salvation of the soul. The account of the paralytic brought to Christ by his friends makes this perfectly clear (Mark 2:1-12). Before healing the paralytic, the Lord informed him that his sins were forgiven. To the opposition accusing Him of blasphemy, Jesus replied that the healing He was about to perform would be proof of His power to forgive sins, confirming that He was indeed the Son of God. The salvation of the soul and the healing of the body are combined here in a two-fold manifestation of the will of God for suffering humanity.

From this incident, we can see still further the relationship between forgiveness and healing. If there is a connection between sin and sickness, it's only logical to expect that forgiveness should be accompanied by a visible sign [healing] of the complete redemption and deliverance from the results of sin [sickness].[1]

Furthermore, when people came in faith to Jesus for healing, He responded without any hesitancy whatsoever. He saw the physical conditions of individuals as opportunities for manifesting the power of God and glorifying His Father (John 9:3; 11:4). All we have to do is look to His example to understand the will of God concerning healing.

Jesus came to earth, not to do His own will, but the will of His Father who sent Him (John 6:38). He further declared, "...My food is to do the will of Him who sent Me, and to finish His work" (John 4:34).

With regard to the witness of John the Baptist, Jesus said,

*But I have a greater witness than John's; for the works which the Father has given me to finish–the very works that I do–bear witness of me, that the Father has sent Me (John 5:36).*

In the case of the healing of the man born blind, Jesus specifically said, "I must work the works of Him who sent Me..." (John 9:4). To his disciple Philip, Jesus declared, "...He who has seen Me has seen the Father;.." (John 14:9). Jesus also told Philip,

---

1. Sickness is not always a direct result of sin. This subject will be dealt with in Chapter Two, under the heading of "Job."

17

*...The words that I speak to you I do not speak on
My own authority; but the Father who dwells in Me
does the works (John 14:10).*

From these statements of Christ, it's impossible to believe
that sickness has ever been the will of God for His people! Jesus'
attitude toward all illness was expressed in a relentless warfare
against Satan. As Jesus healed the sick, He was not only doing the
**works** of God but also manifesting to all mankind the **will** and
**heart** of His Father in heaven.

Furthermore, this section of our study would be incomplete
without remembering that Jesus is the same yesterday, today, and
forever (Hebrews 13:8). The Greek words for the phrase "the same"
are the words "ho autos," which mean the same identical person in
**every** respect. Since Christ is the same as in the past, we can expect
His healing power to be available to us, just as it was to those who
were healed under His earthly ministry.

**The Early Disciples and Healing**

We can be confident that healing is the will of God because
healing was also included in the ministry of Jesus' disciples.
Healing the sick was not exclusively limited to the Son of God. In
the early days of His ministry, Jesus began in a very practical way
to instruct His disciples about the healing of the sick. For example,
when He raised Jairus' daughter from the dead, Jesus took Peter,
James, and John with Him into the room where the girl was lying,
and they became eyewitnesses of the miracle (Mark 5:37-43).

On another occasion, after Jesus had descended from the
Mount of Transfiguration, He found that in His absence the disciples hadn't been able to cast a dumb spirit out of a young boy. Upon

seeing this, the Lord admonished them publicly and said, "... faithless generation, how long shall I be with you? how long shall I bear with you? Bring him to Me" (Mark 9:19).

Later, His disciples asked Him why they were unable to cast out the spirit, and Jesus said, "...This kind can come out by nothing but prayer and fasting" (Mark 9:29).

These two examples clearly illustrate for us the cooperation of the disciples with the Lord in His healing ministry; however, the commission of the twelve makes it even clearer. Matthew said that Jesus gave His disciples

> ...power over unclean spirits, to cast them out, and to heal all kinds of sickness and all kinds of disease (Matthew 10:1).

Christ later said to them,

> And as you go, preach, saying,'The kingdom of heaven is at hand.' Heal the sick, cleanse the lepers, raise the dead, cast out demons. Freely you have received, freely give (vs. 7-8).

Mark wrote that the Lord sent His disciples out two by two and gave them power over unclean spirits (Mark 6:7). Luke indicated that Christ gave His disciples

> ...power and authority over all demons, and to cure diseases. He sent them to preach the kingdom of God and to heal the sick (Luke 9:1-2).

As a result, both Mark and Luke recorded the outcome of Jesus' instruction.

> So they [the disciples] went out and preached that

*people should repent. And they cast out many demons, and anointed with oil many who were sick, and healed them (Mark 6:12-13).*

Luke wrote, "So they departed and went through the towns, preaching the gospel and healing everywhere" (Luke 9:6). All this vividly shows that the healing ministry wasn't restricted to just the **physical** presence of Christ.

It must also be noted that the command to heal the sick wasn't limited to the original twelve disciples. In Luke 10:1 it is stated:

*After these things the Lord appointed seventy others also, and sent them two by two before His face into every city and place, where He Himself was about to come.*

Look at the instructions He gave to them:

*Whatever city you enter, and they receive you, eat such things as are set before you. And heal the sick there, and say to them, '**The kingdom of God has come near to you**' (vs. 8-9, emphasis added).*

For the disciples, as well as Christ, evangelism and healing went hand in hand. It's obvious that the healing of the sick was included in the preaching of the Kingdom of God.

## Healing through the Atonement

Healing was also included in the Father's great plan of redemption. Since sickness entered the world through sin, its only true remedy can be found through the Atonement of Jesus Christ.

According to the classic text on the Atonement, Isaiah said of the Messiah,

> *Surely He has borne our griefs [Hebrew: choliy], And carried our sorrows [Hebrew: mak'ob]; Yet we esteemed Him stricken, Smitten by God, and afflicted. But He was wounded for our transgressions, He was bruised for our iniquities; The chastisement for our peace was upon Him, And by His stripes [wounds] we are healed (Isaiah 53:4-5).*

Many Christians believe that these verses only refer to spiritual healing rather than physical healing. The fact remains, however, that Isaiah 53:4 doesn't refer to spiritual matters but to bodily healing. This can be proven by Matthew, when he said, in quoting Isaiah 53:4,

> *...And He [Jesus] cast out the spirits with a word, and healed all who were sick, that it might be fulfilled which was spoken by Isaiah the prophet, saying: "He Himself took our **infirmities**, and bore our **sicknesses"** (Matthew 8:16-17, emphasis added).*

Here we are given a much more accurate rendering of the original Hebrew text. Every unbiased Hebrew scholar must agree that the words, "griefs" [choliy] and "sorrows" [mak'ob], found in Isaiah 53:4 should have been translated "sicknesses" and "pains," respectively. This is confirmed by Franz Delitzsch,[2] who was one of the greatest modern Hebrew scholars. In his commentary, he translated Isaiah 53:4 as:

> *Verily He hath borne our diseases and our pains: He hath laden them upon Himself, but we regarded Him as one stricken, smitten of God, and afflicted.*

Delitzsch indicated Matthew was faithful to this text in translating it in Matthew 8:17 as:

> *He Himself took our infirmities, and bore our sicknesses.*

Delitzsch further stated that the bearing and subsequent removing of our sicknesses and pains were an essential part of the redeeming work of Jesus Christ.

This can also be seen from other passages of Scripture. For example, in Deuteronomy 7:15, it's stated, "And the LORD will take away from you all sickness [Hebrew: choliy],... " The Hebrew word "choliy" is further translated "sickness" in Deuteronomy 28:61; 1 Kings 17:17; 2 Kings 1:2; 8:8.

On the other hand, the Hebrew word "mak'ob" is translated "pain" in Job 14:22, as well as in Job 33:19, where we read, "Man is also chastened with pain on his bed, and with strong pain in many of his bones."

To suggest that Matthew made an incorrect comparison between Isaiah 53:4 and Matthew 8:16-17 would also be charging the Holy Spirit with making a mistake in quoting His own prediction. Matthew declared Jesus was fulfilling the prophecy given through Isaiah, which says He bore our diseases and pains on the Cross.

In addition, the Hebrew verb "nasa'," translated "borne" in Isaiah 53:4, is the identical verb used in verse 12 of the same chapter to speak of the bearing of sins. In this twelfth verse, the true

---

2. Commentary on the Old Testament by C. F. Keil and F. Delitzsch, Volume 7, Isaiah, pages 315-316.

meaning of the verb "nasa'" is made very clear: "...And he was numbered with the transgressors, And he bore [nasa'] the sin of many, And made intercession for the transgressors."

The word "nasa'" is a Levitical term meaning "to lift up or remove to a distance." It was also applied to the scapegoat which bore away the sins of the people (Leviticus 16:20-22).

This word denotes actual substitution, for the full meaning of the verb "nasa'" means "to bear as a substitute." It speaks of taking the debt and carrying it as one's own, as well as completely removing the thing borne.

How did Christ bear our sins? He bore the punishment of our sins as our Substitute. Therefore, according to Isaiah 53:4, when Jesus went to the Cross, He bore our sicknesses the very same way in which He bore our sins. As our Substitute and as a part of the work of the Atonement, Jesus completely removed our sicknesses and pains. There can be absolutely no other logical conclusion!

In the New Testament, Paul also implied that bodily healing is provided through the Atonement:

> Or do you not know that your body is the temple of the Holy Spirit who is in you, whom you have from God, and you are not your own? For you were bought at a **price**; therefore glorify God in your **body**, and in your spirit, which are God's (1 Corinthians 6:19-20, emphasis added).

The Greek word for "bought" in 1 Corinthians 6:19 is the same word that is translated "redeemed" in Revelation 5:9. Paul states that a Christian's body, as well as his spirit, belongs to God and has been purchased with a price. John declared that Christ redeemed us with His blood. These two passages strongly suggest that when Jesus shed His blood on the Cross, He redeemed us, both body and spirit.

Peter also reinforced the fact that healing is provided through the Atonement by writing that Jesus

> *...bore our sins in His own body on the tree, that we, having died to sins, might live for righteousness—by whose stripes [wounds] you were healed (1 Peter 2:24, emphasis added).*

The word for "healed" used in this verse is from the Greek word "iaomai." This verb is used twenty-eight times in the New Testament and usually refers to physical healing. Inasmuch as the Greek word for physician is "iatros," a noun derived from the verb "iaomai," we can see even more that when Peter said "by whose stripes ye were healed," he was referring to physical healing and not just spiritual healing or blessing.

As we've already seen, every form of sickness and disease known to mankind was included in the curse of the Law (Deuteronomy 28:15-68). Paul tells us in Galatians 3:13 that

> *Christ has redeemed us from the curse of the law, having become a curse for us (for it is written, "Cursed is every one who hangs on a tree.")*

Here it's plainly stated that on the Cross Christ bore the curse of the Law and, therefore, has legally redeemed us from sickness and disease. Healing is not merely an incidental aspect of the salvation of man, but is, in fact, an essential part of Redemption. Whoever embraces salvation by faith in Jesus Christ should recognize that the promise applies as much to physical health as it does to spiritual health.

This can be further illustrated for us if we just look at the full meaning of the word "salvation." In the Greek language, the word for "salvation" [soteria] not only means deliverance from all sin but also refers to physical healing and health. Consequently, the healing ministry of Christ and His work of salvation are inseparable.

When coming to Jesus for healing, let's keep in mind that we're not asking Him to do something unusual for us. Instead, we must understand that He is more than willing to have us share in what He has already provided through His death and resurrection.

## Healing and the Great Commission

In the last words of Christ recorded by Mark, the Lord broadened the range of the ministry of healing. With the command to preach the Gospel to the whole world, He added the following specific promises:

> *And these signs will follow those who believe: In My name they shall cast out demons; they will speak with new tongues; they will take up serpents; and if they drink anything deadly, it will by no means hurt them; they will lay hands on the sick, and they will recover (Mark 16:17-18).*

These promises were not merely limited to those who had the privilege of receiving their instruction directly from the Lord; they were also given to anyone who would believe them. Faith in Christ enables any person to become both a disciple and a witness. Every one of us must realize that we're not only called to preach the Gospel but, in turn, demonstrate the Word through the ministry of the supernatural

Furthermore, when Jesus gave the Great Commission, He commanded that those who believed the Gospel should be baptized in water. In the same commission He commanded **all** believers to minister to the sick by laying hands on them and praying for them. To suggest that all of the Commission was for the early believers but only part of it should be practiced today is seriously tampering with the Word of God!

## Healing Established in the Church

In addition to the Great Commission, Jesus, following His ascension into heaven, placed gifts of healings in the Church (1 Corinthians 12:28) for the continuance of His earthly ministry through His people. Faithful to her mission, the Early Church took the Lord's commands seriously and carried on the ministry of healing to the fullest extent.

The Book of Acts records seven instances of an individual being healed (Acts 3:1-8; 9:10-18, 32-35, 36-42; 14:8-10; 28:3-6, 8), as well as seven other occasions when multiple healings actually took place through the Name of Jesus (Acts 2:43; 5:12-16; 6:8; 8:5-8; 14:3; 19:11-12; 28:9).

This should be sufficient evidence that, for the Early Church, healing wasn't a question or problem to be solved, but a living reality which was never in doubt. Having complete faith in Christ, the apostles, as well as other believers, preached and healed the sick as the Lord Himself had done. For the Christians in the Book of Acts, the only thing that mattered was obedience to the commands they had received directly from Jesus—an obedience that sprang from their trust in Him and in the fulfillment of all His promises.

A study of the history of the Christian Church also confirms that the healing ministry continued for the first three centuries following the death of Christ. Although its importance gradually diminished, it didn't completely disappear. In spite of the fact that during certain periods of time, one can scarcely find traces of the ministry of healing, the fact remains, however, that throughout Church history, including this present age, miracles of healing have been experienced. This only proves that as long as the Church is in existence and in a position to believe, the gifts and power of God will be present to heal the sick.

## Conclusion: God's Will Is Healing

God's will concerning healing is even further revealed by the clear command given in James 5:14-16. In writing the first letter of the New Testament, James clearly stated that those who were sick in the Church should ask for the anointing of oil, with the promise that the prayer of faith would heal them and the Lord would raise them up.

Certainly James is referring here to physical healing because the word for "save" [Greek: sosei] in verse 15 is from the very word Jesus used every time He said to a sick person, "Your faith has made you well." (See Matthew 9:22; Mark 6:56; 10:52; Luke 8:48; 17:19.) Let's ask ourselves: would God command the anointing of oil and prayer for the sick if it weren't His will to heal the sick?

We have seen in this chapter how God's Word is a direct revelation of what He is willing and eager to do for us. Since Christ already bore our sicknesses and pains on the Cross, we don't need to suffer endlessly with them.

If the Father wanted some of us to remain sick and afflicted, Jesus would not have borne our pains and sicknesses on the Cross, for in so doing He would have freed us from the very thing God would have wanted us to bear. Because Christ said, "...Behold, I have come to do Your will, O God...." (Hebrews 10:9), we can be certain that healing is the will of the Father.

Many have attempted to reword the Father's will; yet, a will can never be changed after the death of the one who made it (Hebrews 9:16-17). Before leaving this world, Jesus revealed to us that the will of God included deliverance from both sin and sickness.

If you're in need of healing, lay aside all unscriptural teaching which encourages you to suffer physically with pain and sickness. Read the Father's will–His Word. Make use of its benefits in the Name of Jesus.

Although Satan has blinded the hearts and minds of many from beholding all of the benefits of the Cross, never lose sight of them, because God has not only forgiven you of all your sins, but also healed you of all your diseases (Psalm 103:3)

# CHAPTER II

# Objections to Healing

Although we've seen from the previous chapter the heart of the Father in the matter of healing, there may still be a reluctance on the part of some of us to fully embrace all that has been provided through Christ. This may be due, somewhat, to various religious objections that have been raised in opposition to the message of healing. The fact that some haven't been healed has caused a significant element of the Church to create theories which have suggested there are many exceptions to the promises of healing.

Because the teachings of men have replaced the Word of God, for many people the promises of God aren't effective in bringing about a change in their individual lives (Mark 7:13). The faith of countless Christians has been severely crippled by religious tradition. Instead of having confidence in the finished work of the Cross, their minds are now plagued with a lot of questions.

The purpose of this chapter is not to be argumentative; instead, I want to deal with as many questions and objections concerning healing as possible in order that the faith God has given to every one of us as believers (Romans 12:3) can be released to embrace all of His promises.

## No Healing through the Atonement

Those who don't believe Jesus redeemed us from our diseases when He atoned for our sins would argue that it can be proven that healing isn't provided through the Atonement on the basis of Matthew 8:16-17 which says,

> When the evening had come, they brought to him many who were demon-possessed. And he cast out the spirits with a word, and healed all who were sick, that it might be fulfilled which was spoken by Isaiah the prophet, saying, "He Himself took our infirmities, and bore our sicknesses."

Because of the seventeenth verse and specifically the phrase, "that it might be fulfilled," the question has been raised: "When did Jesus take these infirmities and bare these sicknesses?" Many would suggest that Isaiah 53:4 was completely fulfilled before the Cross during the earthly ministry of Christ and, therefore, this prediction has nothing to do with us today.

If this reasoning is correct, we will be forced to reach several serious conclusions. First of all, we must remember that Jesus forgave sins before the Cross (Matthew 9:2). Are we then to believe that forgiveness of sins isn't provided through the Atonement and likewise not for today? Jesus both healed the sick and forgave sins before He went to the Cross. Therefore, it must be resolved that the Savior both forgave sins and healed the sick on the basis of His future sacrifice and what He would fulfill at the Cross.

Secondly, does the phrase, "that it might be fulfilled," actually prove that the prophecy of Isaiah came to pass prior to Jesus' death? In Matthew 12:14, we read of a meeting held by angry Jews for the purpose of killing Christ because He had healed an individual on the Sabbath. The Lord, in turn, quickly withdrew from the city, even though a large number of people followed Him (v. 15). Matthew went on to relate why Jesus retreated from these men:

> *that it might be fulfilled [Greek: plerothe–the same word used in Matthew 8:17] which was spoken by Isaiah the prophet, saying: "Behold! My Servant whom I have chosen; My Beloved in whom My soul is well pleased! 1 will put My Spirit upon Him, And He will declare justice to the Gentiles. He will not quarrel nor cry out, Nor will any one hear His voice in the streets. A bruised reed He will not break, And smoking flax He will not quench, Till he sends forth justice to victory; And in His name Gentiles will trust (Matthew 12:17-21).*

Here is a prediction taken from Isaiah 42:1-4 which foretold that in the future the Gentiles [nations] would hear the Gospel and trust in Christ and that He would one day come in might and power to destroy all His enemies.

However, Matthew stated that the prophecy of Isaiah was fulfilled during the ministry of Christ, even before the Gentile nations had heard the Gospel. He also used the very same Greek word concerning the fulfillment of this prophecy that he used in Matthew 8:17 regarding the fulfillment of Isaiah 53:4 [Greek: plerothe, first aorist passive, subjunctive, third person singular of the verb "pleroo"–I fulfill].

No doubt the fulfillment of Matthew 12:17-21 will take place in its entirety at the time of the Second Coming of Christ. Yet, here in this passage the Holy Spirit referred to it in another way. Israel had begun to reject Jesus and so the Gentiles were given the privilege of hearing the "good news" of God's gift to mankind.

Why did the Holy Spirit through Matthew state that the prophecy of Isaiah 42:1-4 was fulfilled during his time when some of it would not be completed until Jesus set up His Kingdom on the earth? We are given a clue in Romans 4:17 where we're told that God "...calls those things which do not exist as though they did." Since God isn't bound by time or space, those things which He has purposed in His heart from before the foundations of the world, He has always considered as done. In spite of the passing of time, from God's perspective, all that He has determined is already accomplished and just awaits manifestation.

This is vividly illustrated in Isaiah 7:14, which reads, "Therefore the Lord Himself will give you a sign: Behold, the virgin shall conceive and bear a Son, and shall call His name Immanuel." In the original Hebrew text it actually says, "Behold, a virgin has conceived [is pregnant]." It was prophesied in a form of the verb called the "perfect state," as if it had already happened, even though the prophecy was given seven hundred years before the birth of Christ.

Furthermore, the Greek aorist **subjunctive**, as found in both Matthew 8:17 and 12:17, is commonly used to speak of future events. While the aorist indicative denotes momentary completed past action, it's the aorist subjunctive that expresses future events which must **certainly** come to pass.

Matthew knew that the prophecies of Isaiah 42:1-4 and 53:4 would be fulfilled by God; therefore, he used the aorist subjunctive in his letter to bring out the tremendous truth that their fulfillment was even then guaranteed!

This idea is again seen in Luke 4:17-21:

*And He was handed the book of the prophet Isaiah. And when He had opened the book, He found the place where it was written: "The Spirit of the Lord is upon Me, Because He has anointed Me to preach the gospel to the poor; He has sent me to heal the brokenhearted, To proclaim liberty to the captives And recovery of sight to the blind, To set at liberty those who are oppressed; To proclaim the acceptable year of the Lord." Then He closed the book, and gave it back to the attendant and sat down. And the eyes of all who were in the synagogue were fixed on him. And He began to say to them, "Today this Scripture is fulfilled [Greek: peplerotai] in your hearing."*

The Greek word "peplerotai" is the perfect passive, third person singular of the verb "pleroo" [I fulfill], and is the very same verb found in Matthew 8:17. Therefore, Luke 4:21 should literally read, "...Today this scripture has been fulfilled in your hearing."

Yet, who would be foolish enough to even imply that this prediction from Isaiah 61:1-2 has been completely fulfilled? Jesus is still preaching the Gospel to the poor through His believers. He is still binding up the brokenhearted. He continues to preach deliverance to the captives and give eyesight to the blind.

There is also a portion of this prophecy that Jesus didn't quote, which is yet to be fulfilled; it's found in the latter part of verse 2. Luke, however, was so convinced that one day this prophecy would come to pass in its entirety that he used the **perfect** tense to bring out the fact that its fulfillment was even then assured.

All that we've looked at so far is positive proof that the prophecy of Isaiah 53:4 wasn't fulfilled during the ministry of Christ, but rather, on the Cross; therefore, its benefits are still available to us today.

Finally, if healing isn't provided through the Atonement, why were there "types" of the Atonement found in connection with physical healing throughout the Old Testament? In Exodus 12:3-11, for example, Israel was required to eat the flesh of the passover lamb for life and strength. As a result "...there was none feeble among His tribes" (Psalm 105:37). Although young and old alike made the journey out of Egypt, nothing is said that would even indicate that any died along the way from sickness or exhaustion. This was because they had partaken of a "type" of Christ, who is Life and Strength.

The Apostle Paul told us in 1 Corinthians 5:7 that "...Christ, our Passover, was sacrificed for us." Since Jesus is our Passover Lamb, we can only conclude that His flesh [body] was also broken for our physical well-being. This is pictured beautifully in 1 Corinthians 11:23-27, in what is commonly referred to as the Lord's Supper. The Communion of the bread and cup is more than just an ordinance of the Church. In Christ there is both spiritual and physical life. There is no better time for having our bodies quickened by the life of Jesus than while we're partaking of the elements symbolizing His body and blood.

If Israel could experience physical life and strength through that which typified Christ, how much more can we expect to be brought into a greater realm of divine life and health through our union with Him.

Again, we read from Numbers 16:46-50 that after almost fifteen thousand people had died because of a plague, Aaron as high priest made an atonement for the removal of the disease and the healing of the people. If, under an inferior covenant, the high priest could make atonement for the healing of the Israelites, how much more can we, under a better covenant, believe that Christ as our High Priest, through His Atonement, has removed from us the plague of sin and sickness.

We also have the example of the children of Israel who were all healed as they looked at the brazen serpent (Numbers 21:9), which, according to John 3:14, was a "type" of the Atonement of Jesus Christ. If healing isn't provided through the Atonement, as some suggest, why were these people who were dying challenged to look at a "type" of the Atonement for bodily healing? As the curse was taken away by the lifting up of the brazen serpent in the wilderness, even so Galatians 3:13 tells us that the curse against us has been removed by the lifting up of Christ.

In light of all the evidence presented in this chapter of our study, as well as the section in Chapter One which dealt with this same subject, it should be obvious that healing has been provided through the Atonement!

## The Disputed Text of Mark 16:9-20

There are those who seek to discredit the ministry of healing by suggesting that the healing of the sick isn't a part of the Great Commission and, therefore, has no place in world evangelism today. This argument is based upon the theory that verses 9-20 of

Mark 16 are not authentic and are not found in the older, more accurate manuscripts.

There are four main manuscripts which have been used as a basis for our Greek New Testament. These are known as Codex A, Codex B, Codex C, and Codex Aleph. Two of these manuscripts, Codex B [Vaticanus] and Codex Aleph [Siniaticus], omit the last twelve verses of Mark 16. It's significant that these two manuscripts also omit other important passages. With the exception of these two, there are no other manuscripts in existence which omit these verses.

Why do these two manuscripts omit these verses in Mark 16 when all other manuscripts, the Early Church Fathers, and the versions include them?

Although these two manuscripts are often identified as the oldest and best, they are not good manuscripts. In reality, they represent mutilated, poorly copied texts. The older of the two, the Vatican manuscript, has no recommendation from any ancient authority. One modern scholar admits that it contains hundreds of omissions of words and clauses. [There are seven ancient versions that include these verses which predate the Vatican manuscript.]

The Siniatic manuscript [Codex Aleph] is also full of errors. In many cases, phrases of a dozen or more words are carelessly omitted. The letters of some sentences have been traced over and rewritten. Furthermore, this manuscript shows the work of as many as ten different editors who attempted to correct it and make it as readable as possible. The discoverer of this manuscript said the text was "very rough."

The quotes of the Early Church Fathers can also be appealed to as evidence in determining the text of the New Testament. For example, Irenaeus, a prominent figure in the early history of the Church, quoted the verses in question as a part of Mark's Gospel. It's important to note that Irenaeus was a disciple of Polycarp, who, in turn, was a student of the Apostle John. This is further proof that the disputed passage of Mark 16:9-20 is authentic.

The following Church Fathers also quote this passage as being authoritative and inspired:

Papias [60-130 A.D.]

Justin Martyr [100-165 A.D.]

Hippolytus [170-236 A.D.]

Eusebius [260-340 A.D.]

Ambrose of Milan [339-397 A.D.]

Chrysostum [347-407 A.D.]

Jerome [331-420 A.D.]

Augustine [354-430 A.D.]

Apart from the Vatican and Siniatic manuscripts, we don't have one single manuscript which eliminates these verses.

## "If It Be Your Will"

Others are kept from receiving healing from Christ because they've been taught to qualify their prayers for healing with the phrase, "if it be Your will." There's only one example given in the New Testament of someone asking for healing in this way. In Luke 5:12-13, we have the case of a leper who, in seeing Jesus,

*...implored Him, saying, "Lord, if You are willing,*

*You can make me clean."*

This man wasn't sure the Son of God was willing to heal him. Nevertheless, without any hesitation, Jesus

> *...put out His hand, and touched him, saying, "I am willing; be cleansed." Immediately the leprosy left him.*

The "I will" of Christ dispelled all the uncertainty from the heart of the leper.

Concerning the promises of God, it's impossible to release faith until the "if" is removed from our prayers. Having genuine faith is being "fully persuaded" God will do what He has promised in His Word (Romans 4:21). We're never completely persuaded as long as we're adding "if it be Your will" to our prayers.

Those who still believe we should end our prayers in this way usually cite as an example the prayer of Jesus in the Garden of Gethsemane when He said,

> *...Father, if it is Your will, take this cup away from Me; nevertheless not My will, but Yours, be done (Luke 22:42).*

Yet, this is a complete misunderstanding of the attitude of Christ at that particular moment. Jesus knew the will of the Father. As the Son of God faced the agony and horror of the Cross, the only issue that confronted Him was that of obedience. Would He be willing to give His life in death for the salvation of the lost?

His prayer was not an attempt to know the Father's will about some specific promise; instead, it was a prayer of surrender to do what He already knew to be the Father's will. Using this example in order to justify any hesitation we might have concerning God's will in the matter of healing is a serious inconsistency and misunderstanding of the true significance of Jesus' prayer.

Some might also suggest that Jesus, in what is commonly referred to as the Lord's Prayer, taught us to preface all of our prayers with the words "if it be Your will." This, however, is not the case. Jesus was simply challenging His disciples to pray for His will to be done on earth just as it's being done in heaven (Matthew 6:10). Since there's no sickness in heaven, it must also be the Father's will and desire that there be no sickness among His people on earth.

It has further been argued that God's will isn't the same for everyone. Since all of us have different callings in life [businessmen, housewives, ministers, etc.], some see this as proof that none of us can really be dogmatic about the will of God in some matters. This is to confuse knowing God's will for the calling of one's life with knowing God's will concerning the promises of the Word. The benefits of the Cross were purchased for us and are available to "whosoever believes" (Romans 10:11). It's the Lord's will that we all have what He has provided through the shedding of His blood.

For instance, who would ever pray for salvation using the phrase, "Save me, if it be Your will"? It would be unthinkable! We know our salvation is the Father's will because His Word tells us that "...whoever calls on the name of the Lord shall be saved" (Romans 10:13).

It should be just as unthinkable for us to pray "if it be Your will" concerning the hundreds of other promises God has given us in His Son. 2 Corinthians 1:20 tells us

*...**all** the promises of God in Him [Christ] are Yes,*

*and in Him Amen [so be it], to the glory of God
through us (emphasis added).*

Although each of us will have a unique "calling" and the
direction of our individual lives will vary somewhat, when God
makes us promises in His Word either specifically or in principle,
He expects us to accept them as His will for our lives.

In turn, when it comes to knowing the "calling" God has for
us or receiving specific direction needed in everyday life, it's
absolutely essential and appropriate to pray, "if it be Your will"
(James 4:13-15). For example, I've prayed at different times to
know God's will when seeking the Lord's guidance as far as my
travel schedule has been concerned. It's never wrong to be submissive and obedient to whatever He may have for our lives, especially in matters where the Bible is silent.

Yet, it dishonors God for us to pray "if it be Your will" when
His will is clearly revealed. Remember, God's Word is His will. We
don't need to pray, "Lord, heal me, if it be Your will." Instead, we
can ask for our healing in Jesus' Name because we know that it is
God's will to heal us.

## Sickness for the Glory of God

A prevalent objection today to the message of healing sug-
gests that it isn't the will of God for some to be healed because various individuals have been chosen to suffer sickness for the glory
of God. This argument is erroneously based upon two incidents in
the ministry of Jesus.

1. **Lazarus**. Those who hold to this view always point to
John 11 where Jesus said concerning Lazarus' illness,

*...This sickness is not unto death, but for the glory of God, that the Son of God may be glorified through it (v. 4).*

Yet, what did Jesus actually mean by this statement? Was it Lazarus' sickness, in itself, that would bring glory to God, or was Christ referring to something else?

According to verse 40 of the same chapter, it's obvious that the Son of God hadn't been glorified by what had taken place up to that point. The challenge Jesus presented to Martha makes this absolutely clear! The Lord reminded her of the promise He had made that if she would only believe, she would see [future tense] the glory of God. It wasn't until Lazarus came forth from the tomb by the command of Jesus that He and His Father were glorified. We're told in verse 45 that

*...many of the Jews who had come to Mary, and had seen the things Jesus did, **believed** in Him [emphasis added].*

The praise was given to God for the resurrection of Lazarus and not for his sickness.

2. **The man born blind**. When Jesus saw a man born blind, His disciples asked Him who had sinned, the man or his parents.

*Jesus answered, Neither this man nor his parents sinned, but that the works of God should be revealed in him (John 9:3).*

After reading this verse, many have concluded that this man was born blind in order that God could be glorified in his blindness. However, this is not what Christ was implying at all.

41

If this man were born blind for the glory of God, then Jesus defeated the Father's purpose when He gave sight to the man. This man's blindness was not, in itself, glorifying to God; instead, his blindness gave occasion for the works of God to be manifested in him. God was only glorified when those who knew the blind man suddenly realized that he had received his sight through the ministry of Jesus.

We read in Matthew,

> *Then great multitudes came to him, having with them the lame, blind, mute, maimed, and many others; and they laid them down at Jesus' feet, and He healed them. So the multitude marveled when they saw the mute speaking, the maimed made whole, the lame walking, and the blind seeing: and **they glorified the God of Israel*** *(Matthew 15:30-31, emphasis added).*

It was not their sickness, but rather their healing, which caused the multitudes to glorify the God of Israel.

In Luke 13:11, we read of a woman who had been bent over and crippled for eighteen years. Jesus laid his hands on her, she was made straight, and her first response was to **glorify God**. It's also said of those who witnessed this awesome miracle that "...all the multitude rejoiced for all the glorious things that were done by Him" (v. 17, emphasis added).

Not once during His earthly ministry did Jesus ever say to a sick person who desired healing, "It's the will of my Father for you to remain sick for His glory. " It's inconceivable to think Jesus would say such a thing; yet, it's just as inconceivable to believe our loving heavenly Father is glorified when His children remain sick and afflicted. God is truly glorified when the sick and suffering receive complete healing and deliverance through His Son, Jesus Christ.

## Suffering

There are those who, in seeking to justify the necessity of and complete submission to sickness, try to make the Scriptures regarding the "ministry of suffering" applicable to sickness. One passage they often refer to is 1 Peter 5:10:

> But may the God of all grace, who called us to His eternal glory by Christ Jesus, **after you have suffered a while**, perfect, establish, strengthen, and settle you (emphasis added).

Let's ask ourselves a question: "Is it possible to suffer in any other way than by being sick?"

The New Testament often speaks of the participation of the believer in the sufferings of Christ. Jesus told His disciples they would be hated and rejected by all men. He further said to them that '...A servant is not greater than his master. If they persecuted Me, they will also persecute you....' (John 15:20). The disciples also knew that if they were going to follow the Lord, they would have to take up their cross daily. (Matthew 16:24). Their cross included the opposition that would be unleashed upon them by the unbelieving world. Not once did Jesus indicate, as some believe today, that the cross His disciples would have to bear would be one of sickness.

When Paul listed his hardships in 2 Corinthians 11:23-28, he did not include sickness. Elsewhere, when Paul spoke of fellow-shipping in Christ's sufferings, he was always referring to the opposition and persecution he met in his service for the Son of

God. [Paul's hardships are dealt with in greater detail later in this chapter.] It's this kind of suffering of which Peter speaks in 1 Peter 5:10.

It's also said of the apostles that after they had been beaten for preaching the Gospel and healing the sick, "...they departed from the presence of the council, rejoicing that they were counted worthy to **suffer shame** for His name" (Acts 5:41, emphasis added). How did the apostles suffer? Their suffering was nothing other than persecution at the hands of men.

Peter had much to say about suffering and sought to comfort the believers who were experiencing tremendous difficulties. If we'll read such passages as 1 Peter 1:3-7; 3:13-15; 4:12-16, we'll see even more clearly that it's erroneous to identify, as many do, suffering with sickness. In the New Testament the "ministry of suffering" is always synonymous with persecution and tribulation.

To believe that sickness is the will of God is a serious inconsistency on the part of far too many. Those who hold this view don't feel any sense of guilt in trying to do everything humanly possible to ease their suffering and escape "God's will."

We have seen that when Jesus spoke of sickness, He spoke of it as an evil thing from which He was sent to deliver us. We must come face to face with the truth that Christ bore the penalty for our sins and sicknesses on the Cross, but did not bear our persecution and tribulation–our sufferings.

## Chastisement

Someone may ask, "But doesn't God sometimes chasten His people through sickness?" While God is not the author of sickness, when we continually disobey Him, He may allow His protective

44

"hedge" to be removed from us temporarily and sickness may be permitted to touch our lives. It's during such times that our heavenly Father is really providing us with an opportunity to discover that we are spiritually lacking something of major importance.[3]

Maybe our lives until then had been centered on our work, possessions, or other interests. Yet, at the moment our health fails, we suddenly discover the interest in our work disappears, our possessions are really not the things that are valuable, and our self-sufficiency can't help us. What once occupied our time no longer seems significant.

When we find ourselves powerless, we come to realize the necessity of a deeper relationship with Christ. God, in His mercy, is seeking to preserve us from judgment and, at the same time, bring us back into the way of obedience. Our ears which were once deaf to the appeals of the Holy Spirit are now capable of hearing the voice of God as it penetrates our hearts and convicts us of our sin. As we are willing to acknowledge the cause of the chastening and turn from it, our loving Father will not only reveal to us a new life birthed out of repentance but will also eventually withdraw the chastisement from our lives.

---

3. It has often been said that sickness possesses a great power of sanctification. While we will readily admit that many Christians have emerged out of periods of physical suffering more committed to the Lord, let's be clear that it isn't sickness, in itself, which produces holy living. Growing in grace comes about through a proper response on our part to the chastening of the Lord. Sickness, alone, doesn't produce maturity; as we yield to the conviction of the Holy Spirit, our lives are sanctified and set apart for godly service. Let's never confuse the power which sanctifies [God's Word] with the methods God may use to lead us into the manifestation.

It's clear, however, that God has revealed to us through His Word how chastisement of this nature may be avoided. He tells us in 1 Corinthians 11:31 that "...if we would judge ourselves, we would not be judged." In other words, if we're willing to give God our hearts and walk before Him in absolute honesty and humility as He shows us our sins, He won't have to chasten us.

Remember, healing isn't unconditionally promised to all who merely confess Christ as Savior. Only those who lovingly obey God's Word can expect to walk in God's covenant of healing! It is said in Psalm 25:10,

> *All the paths of the Lord are mercy and truth, To such as **keep** His covenant and His testimonies [emphasis added].*

## The Age of Miracles Is Past

Today we're told that the age of miracles passed away with the death of the apostles. This objection is used to suggest that Christ is no longer healing the sick, and the signs confirming the disciples' ministries were just for the establishment of the Early Church and aren't valid for today. For these statements to be true there would have to be a total absence of all miracles and healings from the time of the disciples up to the present moment. If one miracle or sign could be validated following the death of the last apostle, it would prove that the age of miracles hasn't passed away and that these objections have no merit. Let's do some investigating and see what we discover.

When we look to the writings of the Church Fathers, we uncover abundant evidence of the continuation of the miraculous. We will quote just a few examples:

Justin Martyr [100-165 A.D.], one of the Church leaders of his day, said,

For numberless demoniacs throughout the whole world and in your city, many of our Christian men, exorcising them in the name of Jesus Christ, who was crucified under Pontias Pilate, have healed, and do heal, rendering helpless and driving the possessing devils out of the men, though they could not be cured by all the other exorcists and those who used incantations and drugs.

Irenaeus [115-200 A.D.] testified,

Those who are in truth His disciples, receiving grace from Him, do in His name perform miracles, so as to promote the welfare of other men, according to the gift which each one has received from him. For some do certainly and truly drive out devils, so that those who have thus been cleansed from evil spirits frequently both believe in Christ, and join themselves to the Church....Others still, heal the sick by laying their hands upon them, and they are made whole. Yea, moreover, as I have said, the dead even have been raised up, and remained among us for many years. And what shall I say more? It is not possible to name the number of the gifts which the Church, scattered throughout the whole world, has received from God, in the name of Jesus Christ...and which she exercises day by day for the benefit of the Gentiles, neither practicing deception upon any, nor taking any reward from them. .. for as she has received freely from God, freely also does she minister to others.

Tertullian [160-230 A.D.] spoke of the power of Christ manifested in the healing of the sick, the raising of the dead, the casting out of demons, and even in the restoration of the lepers. He was also quoted as saying,

> ...the clerk of one of them who was liable to be thrown upon the ground by an evil spirit was set free from his affliction, as was also the relative of another, and the little boy of a third. And how many men of rank, to say nothing of the common people, have been delivered from devils and healed of disease.

Origen [185-254 A.D.] stated,

> And some give evidence of their having received through their faith a marvelous power by the cures which they perform, invoking no other name over those who need their help than that of the God of all things and of Jesus, along with a mention of his history. For by these means we too have seen many persons freed from grievous calamities and from distractions of mind and madness, and countless other ills which could be cured neither by men or devils.

Clement [150-215 A.D.] said, in giving directions to young ministers for visiting the sick,

> Let them, therefore, with fasting and prayer, make their intercessions, and not with the well arranged and fitly ordered words of learning, but as men who have received the gift of healing confidently, to the glory of God.

It appears from Church history that the miraculous continued through the third century. Then under Constantine, the Church

48

became flooded with worldliness and corruption and, in turn, lost its purity and faith. Nevertheless, over the following centuries, there were those who remained true to God and saw miracles and healings performed in the Name of Jesus. Whenever there was a revival of purity and faith, there were miracles similar to those of apostolic days. These signs accompanied every spiritual reformation. The Waldenses, Moravians, Huguenots, Friends, Baptists, and Methodists all bear record of this fact.

Listen to the testimony of the Waldenses, who, for many years, resisted the darkness of a corrupt Roman Church:

> Therefore, concerning this anointing of the sick, we hold it as an article of faith, and profess sincerely from the heart that sick persons, when they ask it, may lawfully be anointed with the anointing oil by one who joins with them in praying that it may be efficacious to the healing of the body according to the design and end and effect mentioned by the apostles; and we profess that such an anointing performed according to the apostolic design and practice will be healing and profitable.

The famous Zinzendorf of the Moravians [also called the United Brethren] wrote,

> To believe against hope is the root of the gift of miracles; and I owe this testimony to our beloved Church, that apostolic powers are there manifested. We have had undeniable proofs thereof in the unequivocal discovery of things, persons, and circumstances, which could not humanly have been discovered, in the healing of maladies in themselves incur-

able, such as cancers, consumptions, when the patient was in the agonies of death, etc., all by means of prayer, or of a single word.

With the Protestant Reformation also came a revival of healing. The testimony of Martin Luther's prayers for the healing of the sick is among the strongest of any on record in modern times. He himself said,

How often has it happened and still does, that devils have been driven out in the name of Christ, also by calling on his name and prayer that the sick have been healed?

Luther also saw his friend Philip Melancthon raised up from the point of death, totally healed through his prayers.

John Wesley personally recorded over two hundred testimonies of healings that had taken place under his ministry.

Many other accounts from Church history could be shared to further reinforce the fact that there has never been a time when God has not honored the faith of His people with signs and miracles.

It's never a particular place or time in history that determines the supernatural. As someone has so aptly said, "It's apostolic men that make an apostolic age." Jesus declared, "...If you can believe, all things are possible to him who believes" (Mark 9:23). He never once implied that you had to be born in Palestine within the boundaries of the first century in order to experience the supernatural.

If anything, Jesus clearly indicated from Scripture that there would be an increase, not a decrease, of the supernatural after His departure into heaven (John 14:12). All that He did was the **begin-**

**ning** of what He expected to see fulfilled through His Church (Acts 1:1).

Every generation needs an encounter with the living Christ! Until He comes again, the world will never cease to require a demonstration of His power and glory.

## The Importance of the Body

It has also been argued by some that the message of healing places too much emphasis on the physical body. While I would never suggest that healing is equal in importance to the forgiveness of sins, this objection, however, is totally unfounded. In fact, the biblical message of healing should have just the opposite effect. An acceptance of the truth of healing from Scripture should take away the fear of sickness, as well as the constant apprehension that every little ache or pain might be the sign of some serious physical problem.

On the other hand, think of all the people who don't believe in healing. Many of these individuals are paying a vast amount of attention to their bodies and are living in constant fear that something might go wrong. Some of these same people are the very ones who accuse those who believe in healing of placing too much importance on the body.

In reality, those who believe in healing should be so convinced that their heavenly Father is concerned about what He has made that they should be able to commit their bodies to His keeping without all the anxious cares that seem to plague those who don't believe.

As a result of appropriating the promises of healing by faith, we are in a better position to seek first the Kingdom of God so we won't have to focus so much attention on our physical condition. Having put our trust and confidence in the Lord, we can rest assured that Jesus will mend and maintain what has been committed to Him.

Furthermore, since the message of healing is closely associated with the necessity for holiness, it tends to promote, in a very real way, purity and devotion on the part of the believer. Healing encourages such continuous fellowship with God that the spiritual benefits far outweigh the physical. The teaching of healing can be one of the most powerful checks and balances in the lives of those who have truly received it.

Over the years there have been some serious abuses regarding the message of healing through ignorance, false teaching, as well as through self-appointed "healers" and imposters. Nevertheless, the biblical message of healing exalts no man. It offers no promise to the disobedient, and it gives no life or strength for selfish gratification. Instead, it exalts the Name of Jesus, glorifies God, inspires the heart to believe, and challenges the Christian to holy living.

## Further Arguments Against Healing

Those who insist that some are sick because it's the will of God try to strengthen their position by citing certain examples from Scripture which, they believe, prove that God has chosen some of His best servants to suffer with sickness. It's the purpose of this section to address the reasons for these illnesses and to deal as thoroughly as possible with those cases most often mentioned.

**Job**. There are a number of Christians who seek to comfort themselves in their sickness by comparing themselves with Job. It's

52

true that Job was afflicted with horrible, painful boils that not only covered his entire body but also afflicted him for a lengthy period of time. However, there is one major difference between Job's experience and those who maintain that their sickness is the will of God–Job eventually experienced his healing, while these same individuals, sad to say, often remain sick and afflicted.

God not only delivered Job from his disease but restored to him even more than Satan had taken from him. In fact, the Bible says, "...the Lord blessed the latter days of Job more than his beginning..." (Job 42:12) by giving him twice as much as he had before. (Compare Job 2:7 with 42:10.) Job also lived an additional one hundred and forty years and there is no record he was ever stricken with boils again.

Before leaving our study of Job, it would be beneficial for us to examine the major question continually raised in the book–"Why do the righteous suffer adversity`?" Job lost his family, riches, position and was even been attacked with a loathsome disease. Were his adversity and affliction a direct result of sin, or were there other reasons for his suffering?

The primary purpose of the book is to disprove the theory held by Job's friends and many today that all adversity is a sign of God's displeasure. This theory assumes there is sin on the part of the sufferer (Job 4:7-8).

The Book of Job gives many reasons for the trials of our faith, some of which I would like to mention:

1. **Trials and adversity can have an educational purpose for Christians**. Job learned through his trials the meaning of a deeper, abiding faith (Job 13:15-18). He came to view God as his Redeemer in a more meaningful way (Job 19:25-29). He also came

away from his experience with a greater assurance of life beyond the grave (Job 19:25) and discovered that God is absolutely sovereign in all of His dealings (chapters 38-42).

The purpose of our trials is also for developing within our hearts an assurance, as well as an understanding, of our trust in God (Psalm 119:65-72).

2. **Adversity can be for the purpose of humbling man's pride**. Job had asked God why he, a righteous man, had been allowed to suffer. He was clearly implying by the question that he knew more than the Lord. Yet, God's reply to Job put him in a state of real humility. This was the purpose of the Lord's statements to Job in chapters 38 through 42. Through this divine confrontation, Job not only repented in dust and ashes but also developed a much deeper revelation of who God is (Psalm 39:4).

3. **Adversity can sometimes have a disciplinary purpose**. Unlike Job's other two friends, Elihu had a little more insight into Job's dilemma. He saw the chastisement of a loving Father (Job 33:14-30). This is in complete harmony with the rest of Scripture (Proverbs 3:11-12; 1 Corinthians 11:31-32; Hebrews 12:5-11), as we have already seen earlier in this chapter.

4. **Trials can be for the purpose of developing godly character.** It's through the trials of our faith, as we endure by the Word of God, that we come to experience spiritual maturity and an ever-increasing faith (James 1:2-4; 1 Peter 5:10). Furthermore, when our plans are hindered or upset, God is also teaching us endurance and godly contentment (James 5:7-11; Philippians 4:11-13).

5. **Adversity can be for the purpose of teaching us obedience.** Hebrews 5:8 tells us Christ learned obedience by the things He suffered. This meant He learned through practical experience to

obey His Father. He became personally acquainted with the experience of obeying God through adversity.

Likewise, we learn what it is to obey and be submissive to the will of God through adversity; for we can't really know how we would act in adversity until we find ourselves in the midst of it. Without trials and tests it would also be easy to become slack in our obedience and responsibilities.

6. **Enduring adversity is for the purpose of glorifying God**. We may sometimes find ourselves suffering hardship for reasons we don't understand. It's during such times that we're called upon to rejoice in faith, being assured our patient endurance through the trials glorifies God (1 Peter 4:12-16).

7. **Adversity is the key to inner spiritual strength**. Paul reminds us in 2 Corinthians 12:8-10 that Christ's power is made perfect in our weaknesses. We are to see ourselves strong in the Lord, not in our own abilities. Although it would be easy for us, like Paul, to ask God to take away our trials and tests, sometimes an immediate removal of our problems would be against our best spiritual interest. The grace and power of Christ can't always be adequately demonstrated except through experiences of adversity and trial. Divine strength becomes perfected in us as we learn that God's power and grace are sufficient to enable us to endure without the immediate removal of the trial.

8. **Adversity is for the purpose of sharing in Christ's afflictions.** In suffering persecution and hardship for the Gospel's sake, we, as Christians, are viewed as being in fellowship with Christ (Philippians 3:10; 1 Peter 4:13). The significance of sharing in Christ's sufferings is that we are bearing the hatred and persecution Christ would be bearing if He were still on earth. Though it is His suffering, we have the privilege of bearing it for Him (John

15:18; 2 Timothy 3:12; 1 Peter 2:21). In other words, Christians are to bear the reproach the world has for Jesus. While we cannot add to the Atonement of Christ by our suffering adversity, we are called to endure persecution and hardship for the cause of truth and righteousness by our identification with Him (Colossians 1:24). Philippians 1:29 informs us that

> ...it has been granted on behalf of Christ, not only to believe in Him, but also to suffer for His sake.

We can't have one without the other.

9. **Adversity may sometimes have a hidden purpose**. Although the first two chapters of Job give us insight into why the man of God was suffering adversity, the meaning of Job's problems was hidden from him.

There may be times when we also have to endure hardships without knowing the reason why. However, we have an advantage that Job didn't have—we can look to Job's experience and be encouraged, knowing that on occasion God may allow our faith to be tested just to vindicate His faith and confidence in us. This was the case with Job. Satan had challenged the Lord by suggesting that Job only served Him because He had blessed him. Satan never questioned Job's righteousness, but he did question Job's motives. The devil didn't believe anyone could be unselfish in his relationship with God.

God allowed Job to be tested to vindicate His faith in Job's love and sincerity and to also prove that the devil was wrong. Even though Job was certainly humbled by the experience, he maintained his faith and integrity and never once sinned against God with his lips.

While there have been some who have questioned the patience of Job, they have overlooked the depth of this man's calamities and the nature of his trials. The critics have also neglected to realize that Job didn't have a Bible; neither did he have any of the precious promises to turn to for comfort and encouragement. All he had was his faith in the Lord and what had been passed down to him by word of mouth. In spite of all his difficulties, Job passed his tests and remained faithful to the Lord.

If God would allow our faith to be tested for no apparent reason, would we be willing to love and serve Him no matter what happened? Would we be willing to love Him for His own sake, even if we never received any further blessings from Him? Could He trust us to endure faithfully and overcome in all things?

Let's be encouraged in this–Satan had to get the Lord's permission before he could ever touch Job–and even then God limited him in what he could do and how far he could go in Job's life. This principle is just as true for us! If we find ourselves in any kind of difficulty, we can rest assured that our Father will not allow us to be tested beyond what we can endure (1 Corinthians 10:13). Eventually the Father will say to Satan, "You've gone far enough," and he'll have to leave us alone. It's also comforting to know that God will eventually work all things out for our good in the end (Romans 8:28).

In conclusion, we must understand that suffering adversity may sometimes be the result of sin, but not always. The moral principle of cause and effect [sowing and reaping] can't be forced into a nice, neat, logical system. Although it's true when applied to the whole of society, it's not always relevant in every individual case.

The Book of Job teaches us the danger of conceiving of God as only a dispenser of blessings and punishment. The true solution to these complex moral issues is to be found in gaining a deeper understanding of the infinite purposes of God.

While God allowed a **righteous** man to suffer without explanation, truth triumphed in the end. The Scriptures teach that in the light of eternity it will be the righteous who will ultimately be blessed and the wicked who will eventually suffer (Psalm 37; 73:18-20; Luke 16:25).

**Epaphroditus**. Another case frequently mentioned by those who either question or oppose the message of healing involves Epaphroditus, one of Paul's companions in the ministry. In Philippians 2:27, we read that while in the company of Paul, Epaphroditus became sick, even to the point of death. Yet, at the time Paul was writing his letter, God had already delivered Epaphroditus from his physical affliction. Paul stated that..."God had mercy on him" [God healed him], and Epaphroditus was able to make the long journey from Rome to Philippi, demonstrating by his presence the power and love of God on his behalf.

Paul went on to explain the reason for the sickness of Epaphroditus:

> *because for the work of Christ he came close to death, not regarding his life, to supply what was lacking in your service toward me (v. 30).*

The apostle had been ministering at Philippi and his needs had obviously not been met by the people of the church. Apparently, Epaphroditus took this responsibility upon himself, working so hard that he went beyond his own physical strength and found himself stricken with a sickness that nearly took his life. Even in such a work as spreading the Gospel, it's possible to tax the body beyond what God has enabled it to endure.

All of us have the responsibility of taking care of ourselves by getting proper rest. Because Epaphroditus was negligent in this area of his life, he automatically suffered the consequences for breaking certain natural laws. Nevertheless, after a period of rest, he was able to continue his labor for the Lord.

**Trophimus**. A further objection to the message of healing is taken from 2 Timothy 4:20 in which Paul wrote,

> *Erastus stayed in Corinth, but Trophimus I have left in Miletus sick.*

Various individuals have argued that healing must not be the will of God since Paul left Trophimus sick at Miletus. While the Bible doesn't hide the fact that Christians can get sick, it does promise us healing for our bodies. Furthermore, we must understand that healing depends primarily upon the faith of the one who needs the healing.

In Mark 5:25-34, we read of a certain woman who had hemorrhaged for twelve years. This woman had suffered many things, had spent all of her money on physicians, but had grown worse. Pushing through the crowd to get to Jesus, she reached out and touched His garment and was instantly healed. What made this woman completely whole? According to the words of Christ, her faith had healed her. She would not have overcome the obstacles which made it seemingly impossible for her to touch Jesus if it hadn't been for her faith. On another occasion, two blind men came to Jesus for healing (Matthew 9:27-31). The Savior touched their eyes and the men were able to see. Exactly what opened the eyes of these blind men? After Jesus had touched them, He said,

"...According to your faith let it be to you" (v. 29). It was their faith cooperating with the power of God that brought about their healing.

Faith is essential for receiving anything God has promised in His Word. This fact is stated clearly in James 1:5-7.

> *If any of you lacks wisdom, let him ask of God, who gives to all liberally and without reproach, and it will be given to him. But let him ask in faith, with no doubting, for he who doubts is like a wave of the sea driven and tossed by the wind. For let not that man suppose that he will receive anything from the Lord.*

Since some men of God have been given certain gifts of the Spirit, various individuals in need of healing have mistakenly thought that their only responsibility was to attend those meetings where such gifts were in operation. They have even come to believe that the gifts of healings would take the place of their own faith in God. This way of thinking, however, is unscriptural!

When Paul was in Lystra (Acts 14), he saw a man who was "...without strength in his feet,...a cripple from his mother's womb, who never had walked" (v. 8). Notice, Paul did not immediately pray for this man; instead, he first preached the Word of God. Then Paul, "...seeing that he had faith to be healed, said with a loud voice, "Stand up straight on your feet!" And he leaped and walked" (Acts 14:9-10).

Even though Paul had exercised the gifts of healings on a number of occasions, he knew these gifts, as well as his own faith, were insufficient to bring about this man's healing. Rather, it was the responsibility of the crippled man to believe and act upon the Word he had heard if he were to be healed.

In the case of Trophimus, it was his responsibility to believe for his healing and not merely the duty of the Apostle Paul.

Furthermore, the Bible differentiates between instantaneous healings and those which are gradual. When Jesus prayed for the nobleman's son (John 4:46-54), the Word states the boy began to get well from that hour (vs. 52-53). The ten lepers were healed as they went to show themselves to the priests (Luke 17:11-19). The author has ministered to a number of people who still appeared sick even after prayer. Nevertheless, after a period of time, their healings were manifested. When Paul left Trophimus at Miletum, apparently he was still sick. Yet, it is quite possible that Paul had prayed for him and the healing process had already begun.

**Paul's Thorn in the Flesh**. Perhaps the most prevalent objection to the ministry of healing concerns Paul's thorn in the flesh. The teaching that Paul had a sickness which the Lord refused to heal has led to the erroneous idea that God desires certain believers to remain sick for His honor and glory. In order for us to correctly understand this subject, let's consider exactly what the Bible has to say about Paul's thorn:

1. It is remarkable that this passage, which is unique in Scripture, should be singled out as often as it is from the many passages that show healing to be the will of God. In the Gospels, for example, one verse in seven proves that healing is the will of God. In the Book of Acts, the proportion is one in fourteen. How can anyone cast aside all this evidence by misquoting some verses from the writings of Paul?

2. The expression "thorn in the flesh"–a phrase not new with the Apostle Paul–was never used to depict sickness or disease in either the Old or New Testaments. This phrase, instead, is always

used figuratively in Scripture and refers to the harassment by one's enemies. For example, before the children of Israel entered the land of Canaan, they were warned,

> But if you do not drive out the inhabitants of the land from before you, then it shall be that those whom you let remain shall be irritants in your eyes and thorns in your sides, and they shall harass you in the land where you dwell (Numbers 33:55).

This verse plainly tells us that if the inhabitants of Canaan were not removed from the land, they would become "thorns in the flesh" of the Israelites. This is further illustrated in Joshua 23:13 and Judges 2:3, where the word "thorn" is used in a figurative sense to describe the harassment and resistance Israel would receive from the heathen nations if any were permitted to remain in Canaan.

3. Just as the Old Testament stated in each case what the thorns were, Paul distinctly tells us that his thorn in the flesh was a messenger of Satan (2 Corinthians 12:7). This word "messenger" [aggelos] in the Greek never refers to sickness or disease but always refers to a person or personality. This messenger of Satan could very well have been a demon influencing a person or a group of people, such as the Judaizers.

4. Paul not only informs us what his thorn was, but he also tells us what this messenger of Satan was allowed to do:

> ...a thorn in the flesh was given to me, a messenger of Satan to buffet me [to strike blow after low], lest I be exalted above measure (2 Corinthians 12:7).

After Paul's conversion, God came to a man by the name of Ananias, and said of Paul, "...he is a chosen vessel of Mine to bear

My name before Gentiles, kings, and the children of Israel. For I will show him how many things he must suffer for My name's sake" (Acts 9:15-16). Paul had persecuted the Christians, and now he would be privileged to experience the same persecution for the Name of Christ. The following is a list of harassments and "buffetings" which Paul experienced during his ministry:

> The Jews sought to kill him (Acts 9:23).
> The Grecians tried to slay him (Acts 9:29).
> He was opposed by Satan (Acts 13:6-11).
> He was opposed by the Jews again (Acts 13:44-46).
> He was expelled from Antioch (Acts 13:14, 50).
> He fled from Iconium (Acts 14:1-6).
> He was stoned and left for dead at Lystra (Acts 14:8-19).
> He was beaten and jailed at Philippi (Acts 16:16-24).
> He was mobbed and banished from Berea (Acts 17:10-14)
> He was brought before a judgment seat (Acts 18:1-17)
> He caused a major uproar at Ephesus (Acts 19:23-41).
> The Jews plotted against his life (Acts 20:3).

Paul also mentions other sufferings in 2 Corinthians 11:23-28:

> *...stripes above measure, in prisons more frequently, in deaths often. From the Jews five times I received forty stripes minus one. Three times I was beaten with rods; once I was stoned; three times I was shipwrecked; a night and a day I have been in the deep; in journeys often, in perils of waters, in perils of robbers, in perils of my own countrymen, in perils of the Gentiles, in perils in the city, in perils in the wilderness, in perils in the sea, in perils among false brethren; in weariness and toil, in sleeplessness often,*

*in hunger and thirst, in fastings often, in cold and nakedness–besides the other things, what comes upon me daily: my deep concern for all the churches.*

Paul mentions no sickness or eye disease (ophthalmia)–only persecution. The messenger of Satan was responsible for all these "buffetings," as Paul goes on to explain in 2 Corinthians 12. It's possible that everywhere Paul went this evil spirit worked to stir up the people against him. However, his ministry wasn't overcome or permanently hindered by the thorn in the flesh.

5. The Apostle Paul gives us insight as to why God allowed this thorn in the flesh to buffet him. He tells us the thorn was permitted so he wouldn't "...be exalted above measure by the abundance of the revelations" (2 Corinthians 12:7). Having been given extraordinary spiritual revelations, Paul ran the risk of being "puffed up" with pride and, therefore, needed the "trials" to keep him in a place of humility.

Paul's reason for God's allowing this thorn in his life certainly excludes practically everyone. A person should not claim that his sickness is a thorn in the flesh unless he has received a similar measure of revelation that Paul experienced and, therefore, needs to be kept from being "puffed up" with pride. Since Paul's thorn was no hindrance to his faith for ministering healing (Acts 19:11-12), why should it hinder our faith for receiving healing?

6. When Paul asked the Lord to remove this thorn in the flesh, the Lord replied, "...My grace is sufficient for you, for My strength is made perfect in weakness..." (2 Corinthians 12:9). Paul went on to say,

*...Therefore most gladly I will rather boast in my infirmities, that the power of Christ may rest upon me.*

64

*Therefore I take pleasure in infirmities, in reproaches, in needs, in persecutions, in distresses for Christ's sake. For when I am weak, then I am strong (vs. 9-10).*

Notice the contrast in verse 10 between **weakness** and **strength**. Certain words fit with one another, such as salt and pepper, hot and cold, sickness and health, weakness and strength. The issue here is weakness and lack of strength. If Paul was sick, why didn't he say he was sick? The Bible says Epaphroditus was sick (Philippians 2:25-30); it also acknowledges the fact that Trophimus was sick (2 Timothy 4:20). If Paul had been sick, he would have said, "Therefore most gladly I will rather boast in my sicknesses." Instead, he referred to his "infirmities" as weaknesses. An individual can be weak without being sick. The Lord Himself spoke of Paul's infirmities as weaknesses, not as sicknesses. He said to Paul "...My strength is made perfect in **weakness**..." (2 Corinthians 12:9, emphasis added).

When Paul spoke of his weakness, he was not only expressing the results of his persecution and distress but also the nothingness of his own human strength and his utter dependence upon the power of Christ.

Though Paul was weak in himself, the assaults of his persecutors could gain no victory over him (2 Timothy 3:11). He was able to say,

*...I have learned, in whatever state 1 am, to be content: 1 know how to be abased, and 1 know how to abound. Everywhere and in all things I have learned both to be full and to be hungry, both to abound and to suffer need. I can do all things through Christ who strengthens me (Philippians 4:11-13).*

How many of us have learned that it is when we are most aware of our own weakness that the power of God rests upon us in the greatest measure?

7. Let us also consider several scriptures some use to seek to prove that Paul's thorn was an Asian eye disease which God would not heal. One scripture often referred to is found in Galatians 4:14-15:

> *And my trial which was in my flesh you did not despise or reject, but you received me as an angel of God, even as Christ Jesus. What then was the blessing you enjoyed? For I bear you witness that, if possible, you would have plucked out your own eyes and given them to me.*

These verses cannot be referring to Paul's thorn in the flesh because the manner in which he speaks of this temptation [the use of the Greek aorist tense] makes it clear that the issue in question had ceased to exist. Notice, he spoke of it as the temptation which was in his flesh.

Again, when Paul stated that they would have plucked out their eyes for him, he was merely using a colloquial expression to show their willingness to give him anything he needed. We might use the expression, "I would give you my right arm if it would help."

Some also seek to imply that Paul was nearly blind since he went on to say in Galatians 6:11, "See with what large letters I have written to you with my own hand." The conclusion that has been drawn is that Paul's eyesight was so bad during the writing of this epistle that he had to make each letter very large in order to see what he was writing. However, he was not referring to the size of his handwriting but to the length of the letter he had written to them.

The Greek word for the phrase "how large" is "pelikois," the dative plural of "pelikos." For the correct meaning of this word, let's quote Zechariah 2:2 from the Septuagint [the Greek translation of the Old Testament]: "Then said I, Whither goest thou? And he said unto me, To measure Jerusalem, to see what is the breadth [pelikos] thereof, and what is the length [pelikos] thereof." It is obvious from this verse that the Greek word "pelikois" in Galatians 6:11 refers to the length of the letter and not to the size of the print.

In conclusion, although we are not suggesting that Paul was never sick, we are suggesting that it is impossible to believe his thorn in the flesh was some kind of sickness that God would not cure.

Paul's life furnishes us with abundant proof that God is willing to heal as well as preserve the lives of His people. Think again, for a moment, of the afflictions he endured for the sake of the Gospel–eight beatings, any one of which could have killed him. Yet, God marvelously preserved his life, and he was able to carry on the Lord's work. At Lystra, he was stoned and left for dead, which indicates to us the severity of the stoning. However, the Spirit of God raised him up and he returned into the city and continued his ministry. Again, on the Island of Malta, Paul was bitten by a poisonous snake; but to the amazement of the people around him, instead of dying, Paul was supernaturally healed. The Scriptures further declare that Paul labored more than all the other apostles.

No sick man could have accomplished what Paul did and live to tell about it. Rather than being an example of an exception to the promises of healing, Paul is an outstanding witness to the power of God in preserving and maintaining life!

**Death**. Some sincere Christians, in their zeal for upholding the message of healing, have left the strong impression that if someone exercised enough faith, he would not die physically. However, the Word of God does not teach that a person can exercise enough faith to ultimately escape physical death, unless his life extends to the time when Christ returns for His Bride. True faith can go no further than the boundaries set by the Word of God. The Scriptures place a limit on the length of a human life, and each one of us can only claim sufficient health and strength to fulfill our life's work in service for Christ. The Bible says,

> *The days of our lives are seventy years; And if by reason of strength they are eighty years, Yet their boast is only labor and sorrow; For it is soon cut off, and we fly away (Psalm 90:10).*

There is, however, a biblical example which demonstrates that faith may add a limited amount of time to a person's life. In 2 Kings 20:1-6, God commanded Hezekiah to set his house in order because it was time for him to die. Yet, in answer to Hezekiah's prayers, he was granted an additional fifteen years of life. Nevertheless, when the fifteen years were over, he passed away.

Even if it should be the end of life for an individual, God's Word does not indicate that a person has to die sick and suffering. God, who is the Author of life, does not need disease to bring about death. When He is ready to call His children to Himself, all He has to do is quietly withdraw the life He gave them.

The leaves fall from the trees in the fall after their purpose has been accomplished; they don't need to be diseased or blown away by a storm. In like manner, death should be a quiet passing into the presence of the Lord.

Concerning all that has been said in this chapter, each of us is now compelled to make a choice: will we choose to believe the Word of God, or are we going to allow religious tradition to continue to influence our way of thinking?

If we will let the Word of God have first place in our lives, it will not only drive out the doubt from our hearts and minds but also the sickness from our bodies (Proverbs 4:20-22).

# CHAPTER III

# Why Many Fail to Receive Healing

Although many Christians have sincerely sought healing from Christ, we still have to face the fact that a large number of these same individuals have not been healed. We can't pretend to have all the answers. Only God knows the hearts and minds of individuals. We dare not place the blame on anyone; neither should we accuse any individual of disobedience or a lack of faith.

While we never want to fall into the trap of trying to come up with explanations for every individual case in which a healing was not experienced, we need to be aware of some major obstacles that will prevent healing from taking place.

When a medical doctor begins to treat a particular illness, he seeks to find the cause of the sickness and then tries to eliminate that cause. When we come to Christ for healing, we have to understand that He not only wants to deal with the symptoms but, more importantly, with the cause of the sickness. Before anyone of us can receive healing, we must recognize that there are conditions which accompany every promise. We must also be willing to deal with anything in our lives that may have allowed the sickness in the first place.

## Major Causes of Sickness

**Unbelief.** Undoubtedly, the greatest barrier to healing today is the overall unbelief found within the Church. This is largely due to a lack of proper teaching on the subject of healing. It's one thing for those of us in ministry to argue that our first duty is the spiritual welfare of God's people; it's another thing for us to have nothing to offer the sick except exhortations suggesting that their sickness has been sent to them by a loving heavenly Father.

Neglecting the message and ministry of healing is not only being disobedient to Christ's command to heal the sick, but it has also weakened, beyond measure, the faith and authority of believers. By omitting the ministry of healing, the people of God have lost one of their most valuable tools for experiencing and demonstrating the power of God to their generation.

When the Church over the centuries noticed her faith dwindling and the power to heal disappearing, instead of searching for the problem in herself, she changed her doctrines to suit her weakness. Think of where the faith of the Church would be today if she had humbled herself before God when her lack of power convicted her that something was drastically wrong. If the Church had demonstrated her faith through the healing of men's bodies, many more would be seeking the greater blessing of the healing of their souls. Picture for a moment what could have happened all these years on the mission field had the childlike faith of the people been challenged to embrace the message and ministry of healing.

It's sad that men will not believe that the work which occupied such a large place in the ministry of Jesus is a vital part of the work of the Church today. Without question, the greatest obstacle to receiving healing is the lack of faith among professing Christians. However, before we blame the Church as a whole, we must remember that local churches are made up of individuals and the level of faith will not rise any higher than that of the average member. Are we genuinely concerned about the level of faith among God's people, or do we just wanting to complain about it? We have no right to say anything if we are not willing to do everything we can to raise the standard ourselves.

Therefore, let's never give up the fight against sickness and pain. Although sickness will not be completely eliminated until the eternal state, may we never use this as an excuse for not exercising faith for the healing of our bodies. Since God has given us so many promises concerning what He wants to do for His people, we should do everything possible to see that His Word is fulfilled in our lives, as well as in the lives of others.

**Disobedience**. Another major obstacle to the healing of many is willful disobedience against God and His Word. Although healing can be found in the Scriptures, nowhere in the Bible does God promise healing to those who live a **lifestyle** of disobedience! Again, we read in Deuteronomy 28:58-61,

> *If you do not carefully observe all the words of this law that are written in this book, that you may fear this glorious and awesome name, THE LORD THY GOD, then the LORD will bring upon you and your descendants extraordinary plagues–great and prolonged plagues–and serious and prolonged sicknesses. Moreover He will bring back on you all the diseases of*

*Egypt, of which you were afraid, and they shall cling
to you. Also every sickness and every plague, which is
not written in this Book of the Law, will the LORD
bring upon you, until you are destroyed.*

Someone may say, "But this is Old Testament. As a believer under grace, I'm no longer under the curse of the law." However, any person who claims to be under grace but chooses to continually walk in sin is deceived and has no basis for claiming any of the benefits found under grace.

One of the most misapplied verses in all of the Word of God is Galatians 3:13 where Paul said,

*Christ has redeemed us from the curse of the law,
having become a curse for us (for it is written,
"Cursed is every one who hangs on a tree").*

Some believe this verse means that under the new covenant believers can no longer come under the curse of a broken covenant. While we're not suggesting that those who walk before the Lord in obedience and repentance are under a curse, those who will not allow Jesus to be Lord of their lives, but rather **practice** sin willfully, are not under the covering of grace. They may discover, all too late, that they are under a curse for breaking covenant with God.

Breaking covenant with God is refusing to repent and turn completely away from any known sin. It's having a heart that is inclined toward disobedience. If a person commits a sin but genuinely repents by turning away from it, that person hasn't broken covenant. However, if an individual merely says, "I'm sorry," but doesn't allow the lordship of Jesus to be re-established in the area of his life that was surrendered to sin, the repentance isn't genuine.

74

Something has captured an area of the heart because there is a refusal to deal with the sin. According to the prophet Jeremiah, to ignore the Spirit of God calling us to repentance and to continue to walk in the stubbornness of our hearts is breaking covenant with the Lord (Jeremiah 11:7-10).

Grace has never given us a license to do as we please. We read in Romans 6:1-2,

> *What shall we say then? Shall we continue in sin that grace may abound? Certainly not! How shall we who died to sin live any longer in it?*

Grace has never removed the demands of purity. In fact, grace is the power of God that gives a person the ability to walk in holiness before the Lord.

When we come to Christ for healing, we must let Him diagnose our problem. We must be willing to let the Spirit of Truth search our hearts and bring to our minds anything He sees that needs cleansing and adjusting. If we're not willing to allow this to happen, we have no right to expect healing.

Healing is a way of life; it's a walk of covenant that requires loving commitment not only to the benefits of the Cross but also to Jesus Himself. If we want the Lord to take control of our physical condition, then He must have control of our hearts. We must be willing to live in loving submission and obedience to His will. We must allow Him to make us into what He would have us to be and not merely seek to be delivered from our problems.

If we want to receive God's blessings, we have to be perfectly honest with Him. There can be no secret chambers in our hearts and no corners which we are trying to shield from the light of His presence. The honest desire of our hearts must be for truth, purity and love.

When any sin is revealed to us by the Holy Spirit, we need to be honest and call our sins by their rightful names, instead of merely calling them weaknesses, difficulties, or limitations. Sin is an ugly word, but sickness is an ugly thing! We shouldn't mince words when it comes to both of these matters.

Some of us may need to broaden our definition of sin. The sins we commit in thought and speech are just as serious as those we commit in deed. Sin is not only the rejection of God's holy standards but also the rejection of His love and guidance. Any turning away from Him or any attempt to act in our own wisdom and strength is, by its very nature, sinful.

God is love; therefore, any attitude of heart and mind which is unloving and unkind hinders His perfect work from being accomplished in us. An unforgiving spirit, bitterness of heart, hatred and anger, gossip and criticism are all contrary to love and are sin in the sight of God. The command to do unto others what we would have them do unto us opens up an area that most of us would rather ignore. Have we ever thought it necessary to confess as sin the hurts we may have caused others by not being sensitive to their feelings?

Fear is also in opposition to the love of God, for perfect love casts out fear (1 John 4:18). If we really believe in the promises of God, there will be no permanent room for fear in our hearts and minds. Yet, many regard fear as some natural, excusable weakness or nervous disposition, instead of confessing it as the sin of unbelief.

The greater the place self-will occupies in our lives, the less opportunity there will be for the Holy Spirit to reveal Christ in us.

One of self's most destructive forms is self-pity. Many who have had long standing illnesses have experienced the difficulty of again facing the responsibilities of life, as well as the difficulty of forsaking the attention which was shown them during their period of sickness. At times, it's almost impossible to get people to realize that the real cause of their prolonged illness may be an unwillingness to want to get better. This issue is very hard for some to face, especially when they feel they can't get attention any other way. This sin has been responsible for many psychosomatic diseases and has caused many to become permanent invalids.

Self-pity even tempts us to become resentful toward God. When we pray and don't receive immediate help, we're tempted to blame God. We fail to realize that He can't always give us the blessings promised us until a deeper level of maturity has taken place in our lives. It would be easy for us to walk by faith if everything came to us when expected. Rather than proving that God has forgotten us, these times of testing are really proof that He is maturing and training us for His service.

Self-pity also encourages us to nurse every small hurt or grievance which, in turn, causes us to become depressed and irritable. Self-pity makes us regard ourselves as martyrs. When we find ourselves terribly hurt by criticism or unkind deeds, it's far more comforting to attribute our wounded feelings to our sensitive natures than to admit that our pride has been crushed.

Another matter of concern to God is the issue of dishonesty. Yet, there appears to be some disagreement concerning the actual meaning of the term. For example, while some would be appalled at the idea of stealing something that belonged to another person, these same individuals may feel no sense of guilt in not returning items borrowed from others. Or, what of submitting inaccurate income tax returns to the government? Furthermore, dishonesty is more than out-and-out lying. It can also manifest itself in the form of exaggeration, the telling of half-truths, or by keeping silent and allowing someone to believe a lie.

There's also the area of the thought-life. Meditating on wrong thoughts is just as serious in the eyes of God as wrong actions. To give our minds over to uncleanness and sensuality is just as sinful as committing the acts of fornication or adultery (Matthew 5:27-28).

While it is not a sin to have unwholesome (i.e., lustful, critical, jealous, hateful) thoughts cross our minds, it is wrong to allow these thoughts to take root in our minds or affect our attitudes and actions. Allowing wrong thoughts to remain must be repented of as much as wrong actions (Matthew 15:16-20).

Furthermore, it's insufficient to pray merely for strength to overcome temptation. We must go deeper than this and pray that every ungodly desire, which temptation feeds on, will be uprooted from our hearts. We also need to cry out for a love for God that will motivate us to overcome fleshly attitudes and passions.

We can never have the peace of mind through which the Spirit of Christ can do His work in us as long as we're conscious of some wrong that hasn't been made right (Psalm 66:18; Isaiah 59:1-2; 1 John 3:20-22). This is why the Book of James urges us to confess our faults to one another (James 5:16). To seek reconciliation or to admit that we have been unjust or unloving is by no means easy. Yet, when we have great difficulty admitting our faults, this is strong evidence that pride still exists in our hearts. There is nothing more powerful in dealing with selfish pride than absolute honesty.

All that has been said up to this point is not to imply that "absolute perfection" has to be achieved before we can be healed; however, we have to let Christ see that our heart's desire is to love and obey Him. Loving obedience and faith are the two inseparable requirements for obtaining the fulfillment of any of the promises of God. If we desire to believe, we must obey, because faith implies obedience. God is not a respecter of persons, but He is a respecter of obedience.

**Unforgiveness**. One of the greatest hindrances to receiving healing is unforgiveness harbored in the hearts of Christians. Jesus declared in Mark 11:22-24 that true faith could cause the very mountains to be uprooted and cast into the sea. However, He spoke of a condition which, if not met, could not only prevent the release of such faith but could also cause a man to be denied the forgiveness of God. In verses 25-26 of the same chapter, Jesus said,

> *And whenever you stand praying, if you have anything against anyone, forgive him, that your Father in heaven may also forgive you your trespasses. But if you do not forgive, neither will your Father in heaven forgive your trespasses.*

Most Christians understand the importance of forgiveness, but few have placed as much emphasis upon it as Christ did. He required a heart of forgiveness as a prerequisite for answered prayer. If we harbor resentment or bitterness in our hearts as we pray for healing, we rob ourselves of the very thing we desire.

Speaking of the necessity of walking in forgiveness, Jesus taught His disciples that if a brother sinned against another even seven times in one day, he should still be forgiven. Christ knew many would be inclined to believe that after they had forgiven someone several times, they would be justified in withholding further forgiveness. Notice what Jesus answered when Peter asked,

> *...Lord, how often shall my brother sin against me, and I forgive him? Up to seven times? Jesus said to him, "I do not say to you, up to seven times, but up to seventy times seven" (Matthew 18:21-22).*

Possibly even before Peter could recover from the initial shock, the Lord began to relate a parable about an unforgiving servant. Jesus spoke of a servant who owed his lord ten thousand talents. This servant was unable to pay the debt; but as he pled for mercy, his master was moved with compassion and forgave him. Later, this same servant found another servant who owed him a hundred pence. He took the man by the throat and demanded that he pay all that he owed, but he couldn't pay, so the servant threw the helpless man into prison. When the lord heard of the servant's actions and lack of forgiveness, he gave orders for the merciless servant to be delivered to the tormentors until he paid all he owed. Jesus clearly revealed God's will for us when He said,

> *So My heavenly Father also will do to you if each of you, from his heart, does not forgive his brother his trespasses. (See Matthew 18:23-35.)*

Unforgiveness is extremely costly! This was made real to me one day when I received a letter from a woman who was severely crippled from arthritis. She had heard me say in one of my messages that medical science had proven that arthritis, in some cases, was due to the harboring of resentment and bitterness in one's heart and mind. As she listened to the message, the Holy Spirit convicted her of bearing unforgiveness toward a particular individual whom she felt had wronged her. When she asked God to forgive her for the sin of resentment, she was instantly healed! Think of the years of heartache and pain she could have been spared had she understood the seriousness of not walking in the love and forgiveness of God.

The importance of our maintaining a right relationship with other believers is also clearly taught in the Sermon on the Mount. Jesus said that if one came to the altar with his gift and remembered his brother had something against him, he was to leave his gift at the altar and go immediately and do everything possible to seek reconciliation. It was only then that he could return and offer his gift to God (Matthew 5:23-24). Failure to be reconciled with other members of the Body of Christ is a very serious act of disobedience against the Word of God! Christ even went so far as to say that he who refused to make reconciliation with his brother was to be considered as an unbeliever (Matthew 18:17).

Someone may say, "But you don't understand what has been done to me! Why shouldn't the person who has hurt me pay for all the things they have caused me to go through?"

To "get even" is to bring yourself down to the same level as the one who has wronged you. Revenge is one of the most absurd things to which you could ever yield because it will eventually destroy you!

A person may say, "At least I can have the satisfaction of hating the individual." Yet, we have to realize that anger left unchecked will corrode all other emotions. Trust will turn into suspicion. Criticism will replace compassion and faith will become nothing but a cold, lifeless thing of the past.

In addition to devastating us emotionally, deep-seated hatred can also raise our blood pressure, cause stomach ulcers and even invite a heart attack. It is definitely less expensive to forgive than to resent!

Perhaps there are those who are reading this book who still have deep hurts from the past. Although forgiving others is one of the hardest things we will ever do, it is possible. If Jesus forgave those who unjustly nailed Him to the Cross (Luke 23:34), then we, too, can forgive those who have wronged us.

How does it begin? First of all, forgiveness begins with **understanding**. It's realizing that another person's behavior has its roots in their past, in their hurts and in the difficulties of life that have contributed to the problem they may have with us. There is a cause for every action or reaction. The purpose of understanding is to see the difference between what the individual did and who the person is. Although the individual may have done something wrong, the problem is more complex than just the sin itself.

Understanding is walking in the other person's shoes, seeing things through their eyes, and feeling with them, even though their emotional reactions may be unreasonable. It's going beyond what others do or how they act. It's responding to who they are and what they could become.

Walking in understanding is also being responsible enough to accept our part of the blame for the way things are. We can't always use others as scapegoats and feel justified in blaming them for things in which we are partly at fault.

Secondly, forgiveness consists of **valuing** the life of the individual. Every human being has been made in the image of God! Although this divine image has been marred by sin, every person is still precious in the sight of God. No one is too low or too evil to be an object of Christ's love. Remember, those who have injured us will spend eternity somewhere. We must allow the Lord to love these people through us.

Thirdly, forgiveness also includes **compassion**. By seeing individuals through the eyes of Jesus, we will be able to discern the emptiness and rejection that grips them. When we recognize that these people are precious to the Lord, we will realize that our understanding, love, and forgiveness may be their only link to God.

Furthermore, to love is to do something that will begin the healing process. Forgiveness is always synonymous with **reconciliation**! Whether our love is accepted or not, our goal should be to restore the relationship to what it was before it was damaged.

We may think to ourselves, "But I don't feel anything. I don't feel like forgiving." However, forgiveness has nothing to do with emotional feelings! Forgiveness is an act of the will. Just as one wills to resent, one must will to forgive. As we are willing to forgive, we can expect the feelings to follow. The love of God will flood our hearts and we will be able to minister His love even to those who seem unlovable and unapproachable.

This truth became more real to me when I read the testimony of Corrie ten Boom who was in a German concentration camp during World War 2 because she had concealed Jews in her home. After her release from prison, she encountered one of the guards who had caused her much pain and grief. She found herself confronted with the awesome price of forgiveness! We will quote her story from the tract, *I'm Still Learning to Forgive:*[4]

It was in a church in Munich where I was speaking in 1947 that I saw him-a balding heavyset man in a gray overcoat, a brown felt hat clutched between his hands. One moment I saw the overcoat and the brown hat, the next, a blue uniform and a visored cap with its skull and cross-bones.

Memories of the concentration camp came back with a rush: the huge room with its harsh overhead lights, the pathetic pile of dresses and shoes in the center of the floor, the shame of walking naked past this man. I could see my sister's frail form ahead of me, ribs sharp beneath the parchment of skin.

Betsie and I had been arrested for concealing Jews in our home during the Nazi occupation of Holland. This man had been a guard at Ravensbruck concentration camp where we were sent.

Now he was in front of me, hand thrust out: "A fine message, fraulein! How good it is to know that, as you say, all our sins are at the bottom of the sea!"

It was the first time since my release that I had been face to face with one of my captors and my blood seemed to freeze.

"You mentioned Ravensbruck in your talk," he was saying. "I was a guard there. But since that time," he went on, "I have become a Christian. I know that God has forgiven me for the cruel things

I did there, but I would like to hear it from your lips as well. Fraulein—" again the hand came out—"will you forgive me?"

---

4. Good News Publishers, Westchester, Illinois 60153.

And I stood there–and could not. Betsie had died in that place–could he erase her slow terrible death simply for the asking?

It could not have been many seconds that he stood there, hand held out, but to me it seemed hours as I wrestled with the most difficult thing I had ever had to do.

For I had to do it–I knew that. The message that God forgives has a prior condition: that we forgive those who have injured us. "If you do not forgive men their trespasses," Jesus says, "neither will your Father in Heaven forgive your trespasses."

Still I stood there with the coldness clutching my heart. But forgiveness is an act of the will, and the will can function regardless of the temperature of the heart. "Jesus, help me!" I prayed silently. "I can lift my hand. I can do that much. You supply the feeling." And so woodenly, mechanically, I thrust my hand into the one stretched out to me. And as I did, an incredible thing took place. The current started in my shoulder, raced down my arm, sprang into our joined hands. And then this healing warmth seemed to flood my whole being, bringing tears to my eyes.

"I forgive you brother!" I cried "With all my heart!"

For a long moment we grasped each other's hands, the former guard and former prisoner. I had never known God's love so intensely as I did then.

Like Come ten Boom, we will need all the strength we can obtain from Christ in order to love and forgive. Yet, there is a secret that if acted upon will revolutionize our lives and thinking. That secret is this: we cannot genuinely pray for someone and hate them at the same time. The more we will earnestly pray for the one who has wronged us, the more the Father will be able to remove the "sting" of the hurt until we will be able to love without any strings attached. The key is letting God work within us so that we, in turn, can work out His love and forgiveness in everyday experience. We will then come to understand that the primary purpose of forgiveness is not inner peace for ourselves but concern for the relationship and the pain the other person is experiencing.

We must also understand that **forgetting** is the end result of true forgiveness. To imply, "I can forgive but I can't forget" is to misunderstand the nature of forgiveness. Although we may remember the hurtful experience, forgiveness will choose not to relive it. It will not allow a constant rehashing of past hurts or the holding of someone's past over his head. In forgiving, we must give up the demands for perfect behavior on the part of those who have wronged us. We must lay aside all self-righteousness and realize that we are all fallible human beings in need of forgiveness.

Forgiveness will require the rebuilding of trust even at the risk of being open and vulnerable to hurt. It will choose to suffer additional rejection for the sake of seeking to restore the relationship. If Christ has been so longsuffering and kind toward us in forgiving us innumerable times, how much more should we be willing to walk in forgiveness on behalf of others.

**The Occult**. Another obstacle to receiving healing is involvement in the occult. It is at this point that we wish to quote

*Occult Oppression and Bondage (How to be set free)* by H. E. Freeman:

> WHAT IS OCCULTISM? Stated concisely, it is participation or involvement in any way with fortunetelling, magic practices, spiritism, or false religious cults and teachings.
>
> The Scriptures warn that there will be a great increase in occult activity in the last days:
>
> *Now the Spirit speaketh expressly, that in the latter times some shall depart from the faith, giving heed to seducing spirits, and doctrines of devils.*
>
> There has never been a time in history when the warnings against the dangers of occultism were more necessary than in the present. Multitudes of people, Christian and non-Christian alike, find themselves suffering physical, mental, psychic and spiritual oppressions, few realizing that it is because they have allowed themselves to become ensnared in the diabolical web of occult-ism, which is under the influence and control of the powers of darkness.
>
> ### VITAL QUESTIONS TO CONSIDER
>
> If you have ever been involved in any way in the following occult practices, whether done innocently or not, are you aware that the Scriptures condemn such practices without reservation and that you have opened the door to oppression or bondage to the powers of darkness?
>
> Have you ever visited a fortuneteller? Has anyone

read your palm or told your fortune by the use of cards, tea leaves, crystal ball, ouija board, or other means?

Have you consulted the ouija board (out of curiosity or in earnest), or played with the popular occult games being sold today: ESP, Telepathy, Kabala, Horoscope, Clairvoyant, Voodoo, and so on?

Divining for water, oil, minerals, underground sewer and water lines, by using a forked stick or other objects, is an ancient occult practice known as "water witching" or "dowsing. " Have you, or has anyone for you, engaged in this?

Have you at any time consulted a medium, or anyone with psychic or clairvoyant powers? Have you attended a seance or spiritualist meeting, or attempted to communicate with the dead or so-called spirit "guides"?

Have you practiced or experimented with ESP, telepathy, automatic writing, table-tipping, levitation of objects, yoga, PK, remote influence of the subconscious mind of others, or self-hypnosis? Have you been hypnotized?

When ill, have you sought (or were you subject to as a child) treatment or healing of diseases, burns, sickness, wart removal, etc. , through magic charming, powwow, Spiritualism, Christian Science, or by anyone who practiced psychic, spirit or metaphysical healing, or who used hypnosis, the pendulum, or trance for diagnosis or treatment?

Do you read the horoscope columns or follow astrology? Do you read or possess occult literature (books on ESP, reincarnation, dreams, fortunetelling, astrology, metaphysics, self-realization, magic, clairvoyance, hypnosis, yoga, handwriting analysis, religious cults, or works by such authors as Edgar Cayce, Jeane Dixon, Arthur Ford, or Ruth Montgomery)?

Have you ever attended meetings or assented to the teachings of the Rosicrucians, Spiritualists, Mormons, Christian Scientists, Unity, Baha'i, Theosophy, Inner Peace Movement, Spiritual Frontiers Fellowship, Association for Research and Enlightenment, Religious Research Foundation of America, Unitarians, Jehovah's Witnesses, or others of an occult nature?

Do you know that all such occult practices are condemned by God in the Scriptures, being an abomination unto Him and are under His curse? Are you aware that anyone who has ever practiced or participated in any form of occultism (whether done innocently or not) has opened the door to oppression by the powers of darkness, even though such occult activity may have occurred many years ago or before you became a Christian? You may even now be the victim of occult bondage and oppression because of this and unaware of the source and cause of your problems, whether physical, mental, psychic, spiritual, marital or other.

## OCCULT INVOLVEMENT IS IN
## DISOBEDIENCE TO GOD'S WORD

All forms of fortunetelling, spiritism, magic practices, and involvement in the cults and their teachings are absolutely forbidden by the Scriptures:

*...thou shalt not learn to do after the abomination of those nations. There shall not be found with thee any one...that useth divination (fortunetelling), or an observer of times (soothsayer), or an enchanter (magician), or a witch (sorceress), or a charmer (hypnotist), or a consulter with familiar spirits (medium possessed with a spirit "guide "), or a wizard (clairvoyant or psychic), or a necromancer (medium who consults the dead). For all that do these things are an ABOMINATION unto the Lord! (Deut. 18:9-12.)*

The Scriptures condemn all forms of occultism as sorcery and warn that "...they which do such things shall not inherit the kingdom of God" (Gal. 5:19-21), but "...are an abomination unto the Lord" (Deut. 18:12), and "...shall have their part in the lake which burneth with fire and brimstone" (Rev. 21:8). From earliest times God forbade occultism as spiritually defiling (Lev. 19:31), and made participation in it punishable by death (Ex. 22:18; Lev. 20:27), and cause for rejection of that soul by God (Lev. 20:6). (See also: Ex. 7:11-12 with 2 Tim. 3:8; Ex. 22:18; Lev. 19:26, 31; 20:6; 1 Sam. 15:23; 28:3; 2 Kgs. 21:5-6; 2 Chron. 33:6; Isa. 2:6; 8:19; Jer. 27:9-10; Zech. 10:2; Mal. 3:5; Acts 8:9f.; 16:16f.; 19:19; 1 Tim. 4:1.)

## OCCULT INVOLVEMENT BREAKS
## THE FIRST COMMANDMENT
## AND INVOKES GOD'S CURSE

There are but two sources of hidden information and knowledge, or supernatural help, guidance and healing–God or Satan. One may, through prayer in Jesus' Name, seek such help from God. But there is another way to obtain the desired guidance or help–Occultism. Behind this door stand Satan and the powers of darkness who work through the occult media of fortunetelling, magic, spiritism, and false religious cults. The Scriptures forbid man to seek help from or contact with these sources, for it is tantamount to calling upon another god (Ex. 20:3-5)! Satan is called the "god of this world" (2 Cor. 4:4). Although Satan often accommodates the victim with hidden knowledge or help through these sources, this individual has opened a door of access to him and becomes prey to the forces of darkness to oppress in many ways.

The seriousness of occult participation is seen in the judgment of God which fell upon King Saul who died for seeking help from a medium! Read 1 Samuel 28 and 1 Chronicles 10:13-14.

## CHARACTERISTICS OF OCCULT
## OPPRESSION AND SUBJECTION

The following are a few of the evidences of occult oppression or bondage, although some of these symptoms may stem from other causes. Usually when one or more of these manifestations are present, it is an indication of the presence and activity of demonic spirits, as well as the need of deliverance.

Prolonged depression or gloominess; indifference; irresponsibility; unpredictable behaviour; delusions; uncontrollable passions and appetites; sexual perversions; enslavement to drugs, alcohol, or tobacco; compulsive eating; uncontrollable temper, hate, or other psycho-pathic tendencies.

Chronic fear or anxieties; nervousness or neurotic behaviour; feelings of inadequacy or self-pity; abnormal desire for attention; extremely negative personality; compulsions (lying, stealing, gambling) or obsessions (fear of dying; acute jealousy); thoughts of self-destruction.

Psychic experiences; possession of psychic or extrasensory powers (none of which are to be confused with genuine gifts of the Holy Spirit); psychic oppression (seeing apparitions; hearing voices; poltergeist phenomena, etc.).

Indifference to spiritual things, the Scriptures or prayer; chronic doubts and difficulty in exercising faith; unscriptural religious beliefs or practices; inability to receive Christ or the Holy Spirit; hatred of the blood Atonement, blasphemous thoughts against God.

Abnormal talkativeness or loudness; muttering to oneself; shunning others; unkempt appearance; abnormally bright or glazed eyes; sullen, perverse or defiant facial expression.

**Chronic physical ailments that do not respond to prayer or treatment;** serious marital or parental problems; strife and discord in the church [emphasis added].

## METHOD OF LIBERATION
## FROM OCCULT OPPRESSION
## AND SUBJECTION

If the oppressed are to be set free, some Christians must rid themselves of the naive and unscriptural notion that believers cannot be oppressed by Satan. On the contrary, many have been oppressed, vexed, depressed, deceived, bound and afflicted, especially when there has been any occult involvement, whether before or after conversion (See Job 1-2; Lk. 13:11f.; 22:31-32; 2 Cor. 12:7; 1 Thess. 2:18; 1 Tim. 4:1; 1 Pet. 5:8-9; Eph. 6:11-12).

### 1. Confession of faith in Christ.

Without such a confession, there can be no permanent liberation, for where no sincere commitment to Christ is made there is no secure basis for such individuals to make continued resistance to the powers of darkness.

### 2. Confession of occult sins.

All occult involvement must be recognized as disobedience to God, repudiated, and confessed as sin. The oppressed should name each form of occult participation which can be recalled (such as visiting fortunetellers, playing with Ouija board, following astrology, etc.), confessing it as sin, and asking forgiveness in Jesus' Name. It is well to ask pardon also for any occult involvement you may have forgotten.

### 3. Renunciation of Satan and command to depart.

This is not to be a prayer, but **a direct command to Satan himself** by the person seeking deliverance. At this point Satan will only heed a command to depart (at least permanently) from the individual who granted him access in the first place through occult involvement. **In faith, renounce him and all his work in your life and command him to depart in Jesus' Name!**

In exceptional cases where oppression is severe and faith is weak, it may be advisable to have another exorcise these powers of darkness after the first three steps have been taken on the part of the oppressed.

Accept the fact of your liberation **by faith**. Do not rely on "feelings" or "appearances" at this point. Stand on the Word of God–the evidence and assurance will follow. Satan knows that he must release his victim when commanded to do so in Jesus' Name, but this does not mean that the evidence is always seen immediately. Boldly confess your deliverance by faith and "resist the devil and he will flee from you" (Jam. 4:7).

**Demonic Oppression.** As has been shown in the last section of our study, some Christians are not healed because their affliction is the direct result of demonic activity from which they must be delivered. This can be reinforced by looking at the earthly ministry of Jesus.

> *As they went out, behold, they brought to Him a man, mute and demon-possessed. And when the demon was cast out, the mute spoke. And the multitudes marveled, saying, "It was never like this in Israel"* (Matthew 9:32-33)

On another occasion,

> *...a man came to Him, kneeling down to Him and saying, "Lord, have mercy on my son, for he is an epileptic and suffers severely; sore vexed: for he often falls into the fire and into the water. So I brought him to Your disciples, but they could not cure him." Then Jesus answered and said, "O faithless and perverse generation, how long shall I be with you? how long shall I bear with you? Bring him here to me." And Jesus rebuked the demon; and it came out of him; and the child was cured from that very hour* (Matthew 17:14-18).

Jesus didn't pray for the healing of a disease; instead, He cast out a spirit and as He did so, the boy was cured.

This brings us to the question, "Can a Christian be influenced by the powers of darkness?" Yes, believers can be **oppressed** by demonic spirits.

The physical affliction of **righteous** Job was the work of the devil (Job 2:7). In Luke 13:11-16, we note again the account of a woman who was physically oppressed by Satan. According to this passage, she was "a daughter of Abraham" [a child of God], afflicted with a "spirit of infirmity." When Jesus laid His hands upon her, the evil spirit left, "and immediately she was made straight, and glorified God."

Jesus "rebuked" the fever in Peter's mother-in-law and she was instantly healed (Luke 4:38-39). Obviously, Jesus was addressing a spirit causing the fever because no one rebukes a mere rise in temperature. Christ used this same term to rebuke Satan in Mark 8:33 and evil spirits in Mark 9:25.

Scripture teaches that sickness is due to the oppression of the devil:

> *...God anointed Jesus of Nazareth with the Holy Spirit and with power, who went about doing good and healing all who were oppressed by the devil...(Acts 10:38).*

Any Christian who is sick is, to some degree, suffering a form of oppression. If people are to be set free, the idea that believers can't be oppressed by the powers of darkness must be reevaluated.

I'm acquainted with a woman who was suffering from severe back problems and poor eyesight. When it was discovered that prior to her conversion to Jesus Christ she had participated in Yoga and eastern meditation, she received deliverance and the spirits that had been oppressing her because of this ungodly activity were cast out. Immediately her back was healed, and her eyesight was restored to normal!

Through my own personal experiences and studies, I've discovered that the following illnesses and conditions are sometimes caused by evil spirits:

Allergies, arthritis, asthma, blindness, bloating, cancer, cramps, cysts, deafness, dumbness, epilepsy [seizures], fever, heart disease, mental illness of various forms, migraine headaches, pain, paralysis, sinus infection, sterility, and stroke. I also believe that malignant growths are the result of demonic activity. Furthermore, there can be hereditary [physical] problems passed down from generation to generation that will need to be addressed and dealt with through the blood of Jesus.

When claiming a healing, it's important that we be sensitive to the leading of the Holy Spirit in directing us to any area of oppression that may need to be challenged by the authority of the Name of Jesus.

**Fear**. Fear is yet another open door through which Satan can attack the believer. It's not only the cause of many illnesses but also prevents many Christians from being healed.

Various chronic physical problems are reinforced and maintained by fear. As soon as certain symptoms appear, there's usually a fearful expectation that they will lead to something worse. For example, a sore throat or running nose is always expected to precede a cold; therefore, given enough time, the symptoms usually develop into the real thing. Why? Because we expected them to!

Over time, a thought pattern will be established in our subconscious minds which will only need the acceptance of a suggestion to set it into motion. For instance, we may have been taught that sitting in a draft or going out in the cold with wet hair will always result in catching a cold, and so anytime we find ourselves in a draft or outside with our hair still damp, we expect the worst! It reminds us of what Job said of his circumstances: "For the thing I greatly feared has come upon me, And what I dreaded has happened to me" (Job 3:25).

There are those who have lost their healing because fear caused them to expect the return of the former symptoms or illness, and, as a result, what seemed inevitable to them happened.

If we're going to live above the influence of fear, we first have to admit that fear is really the outcome of failing to believe the promises of God. Fear is something that needs to be repented of and then resisted because "...God has not given us a spirit of fear; but of power and of love and of a sound mind" (2 Timothy 1:7). Our faith will never develop and triumph over fear if we're not willing to act on the Word of God.

Furthermore, if a fear has become persistent or recurrent, it can't be overcome by sheer willpower alone. We will have to look to the Lord for deliverance and believe that the Holy Spirit will uproot the fear from our lives. However, even after prayer, the fear may try to come back, especially in the form of thoughts. If we begin thinking that the fear has not gone, we will find ourselves in its grip all over again. On the other hand, if we believe our prayer for deliverance was answered and the fear was uprooted, we will be able to face it merely as a temptation and resist it in Jesus' Name. As we submit more and more to the Word of God, the fear will have no power to control us.

**Wrong Thinking**. Approximately three thousand years ago King Solomon wrote by the inspiration of the Holy Spirit,

> *For as he thinks in his heart [mind], so is he...(Proverbs 23:7).*

Later, Christ reinforced this same truth when He taught that our behavior and even our speech are governed by our hearts–our minds (Luke 6:45).

It's our way of thinking that so often makes us what we are! Unfortunately, many professing Christians have developed harmful patterns of thinking which have robbed them of their peace, joy and even health.

Doctors and hospitals have more patients than they can care for because far too many people are suffering from psychosomatic illnesses which are a result of mental and emotional turmoil.

The mind exerts a tremendous influence over the body! The nervous system, circulatory system, respiratory system and the various secretions of the glands are all affected by our emotions. These, however, are regulated and controlled by our **thoughts**.

For instance, what happens to us when we get upset? The blood rushes to our brains, our heart starts pounding and we usually do something we would never do if we were not upset.

This truth can be reinforced even further by using several other illustrations. For example, what would happen if a person was playing a certain kind of wind instrument and someone stood in front of him eating a lemon? The musician's mouth would begin to water and it would become difficult, if not impossible, for him to play the instrument.

Why would this take place? Because the eyes of the musician would telegraph a message to his brain that someone in front of him was eating a lemon. His mind would immediately send word to his salivary glands and they would begin to function as if the lemon juice were in his mouth.

Or suppose someone had a slight toothache but decided to sit down in a comfortable chair and read a book. If the story was exciting, this person's mind would become so occupied with the thrilling details that the toothache would be forgotten. When the story was concluded, the person's tooth would almost immediately start to hurt again. While he was reading, the condition of his tooth was just the same as before, but because his mind was completely absorbed in something other than his physical condition, he was not conscious of the dull pain that was there all the time.

When a doctor takes someone's pulse, he generally makes some allowance for the self-consciousness of the individual who is being examined. It's a known fact that by thinking about the heart, listening to it pulsate, and counting its beats, a person can disturb its rhythmic action.

This same principle is true concerning our digestive systems. The process of dissolving and chemically changing food in the stomach so that it can be absorbed by the blood and provide essential nutrients for our bodies can easily be affected by our thoughts and emotions.

Some within the medical profession have even suggested that all of the secretions of the body are continually purified or poisoned by the emotions which govern our inner lives.

Ungodly thoughts and attitudes will also cause harmful reactions in every cell of our bodies. Thoughts of fear, worry, jealousy, resentment, anger, and self-pity will not only produce stress but will gradually pollute our systems (Matthew 15:17-20). Anger alone can actually stop digestive action and upset the kidneys and colon at the same time.

As Christians, it's imperative that we change our way of thinking and bring our thoughts into conformity to the Word of God. We dare not allow our minds to dwell continually on our physical condition for this will only make matters worse. The majority of people today are much too inclined to talk about their illnesses and discuss their symptoms with others. Little do they realize the harm they are doing to themselves by keeping their minds filled with thoughts of sickness rather than filling their minds with the promises of God. If the mind is always thinking about some physical ailment, one can hardly expect the condition to improve and the body to mend.

Satan works through the mind, always seeking to implant thoughts that contradict and oppose the truth of God's Word. This is the reason why we must cast down every ungodly imagination and bring our thoughts in line with the Scriptures (2 Corinthians 10:4-5). This is reiterated again by the apostle Paul in Philippians 4:8-9:

> *Finally, brethren, whatever things are true, whatever things are noble, whatever things are just, whatever things are pure, whatever things are lovely, whatever things are of good report, if there is any virtue, and if there is anything praiseworthy—meditate on these things. The things which you learned and received and heard and saw in me, these do, and the God of peace will be with you.*

If we're to know true peace of mind and victory over the powers of darkness in all areas of our lives, we must continually renew our minds through the Word of God (Romans 12:1-2), for our hearts and minds will only give back to us what we put into them.

Our minds are like gardens which will produce either precious flowers or weeds, depending upon the kind of seed sown and the amount of time spent cultivating the garden. Every thought is a seed sown and will eventually produce some kind of fruit. If we're sowing the seeds of the Word of God and are watering them with faith and prayer, the desired fruit will be produced. On the other hand, if we allow unwholesome thoughts of any kind to take root in our minds, they will, like weeds, choke the precious life of God's Word.

Therefore, it's of the utmost importance that we immediately pull up the "weeds" and replace them with thoughts of faith, hope, love, joy and healing. Although the process of cultivating the garden of one's mind takes real discipline, the end result will be well worth it!

**Self-Effort**. Some of us are not healed because there is more self-effort exhibited in our lives than simple, childlike trust. When our healing isn't manifested as quickly as we had expected, we often feel that something more must be done than simply believing the promises of God. We may try a different method of prayer, or seek out another person to pray for us, or even make an attempt to fast. While all these things may be good in themselves, if we do them with the idea of winning healing from God, our efforts will be unprofitable.

Healing can't be won or purchased; it must be accepted as God's free gift. Therefore, having prayed for our healing, we must act as if we've received (Mark 11:24), rather than strive to obtain it.

**Not Discerning the Lord's Body**. Some Christians are not healed because they have not properly discerned the body and blood of the Lord Jesus Christ. In writing to the Church at Corinth about partaking of the Communion of the bread and cup, Paul said,

*Therefore whoever eats this bread or drinks this cup of the Lord in an unworthy manner will be guilty*

*of the body and blood of the Lord. But let a man exam-*
*ine himself, and so let him eat of the bread and drink*
*of the cup. For he who eats and drinks in an unworthy*
*manner eats and drinks jugdment to himself, not dis-*
*cerning the Lord's body. For this reason many are*
*weak and sick among you, and many sleep [die]*
*(1 Corinthians 11:27-30).*

Here was a church that believed in healing and had incredible manifestations of the gifts of the Spirit in their midst. Yet, a large number of these people were sick and many had even died prematurely. What was the reason for such a tragedy? Paul clearly said it was because the people had partaken of Communion in an unworthy manner and had brought judgment upon themselves.

What was Paul referring to when he wrote of those who partook of the Communion of the bread and cup unworthily? Was he referring to their own personal worthiness before God? Of course not! No man, in himself, is worthy of any of the Lord's favors or benefits. Only Jesus can make a man worthy through His blood.

Instead, Paul was speaking of those who had refused to repent when confronted with the seriousness of their sin and, therefore, had judged themselves as being unworthy of the body and blood of the Lord Jesus Christ.

Many of the people had become divided over various issues, and some, in particular, were quite contentious (1 Corinthians 1:10-11; 3:3). Certain individuals had committed gross sins against other Christians (1 Corinthians 5:1-5). Some had taken others within the church to court (1 Corinthians 6:1-8). This strife and carnality was even carried over into the taking of Communion (1 Corinthians 11:17-21). It was in this context that Paul said,

*For he who eats and drinks in an unworthy manner eats and drinks judgment to himself, not discerning the Lord's body. **For this reason many are weak and sick among you, and many sleep** (vs. 29-30, emphasis added).*

These Corinthian believers had failed to realize that they couldn't sin against one another [the Body of Christ] with impunity. They had neglected to see Christ in their brothers and sisters and, therefore, couldn't comprehend that in sinning against one another they had actually sinned against the Lord.

This is the law of the Body–to speak against other Christians in a local church or elsewhere is to speak against Christ. To harm other believers in any way is to touch the Lord in an ungodly manner. To even withhold love from others is to withhold the same from Christ (Matthew 25:34-45).

This is a divine principle that should grip every one of our hearts. The sickness that is so prevalent in the Church today is due, in large part, to the diseased relationships within its walls! When are we as God's people going to realize that where there is division, criticism, and ungodly judgment, there will also be present every evil work? These sins will open the floodgates of demonic activity into our lives, as well as our churches.

We can no longer afford to justify any form of gossip or criticism under the guise of "discernment," whether it be toward leadership (Numbers 12:1-9) or various members of the Church.

Even if there are differences among fellow-Christians, there is never any excuse for ungodly attitudes or actions. We have been called to bless and not curse–to overcome evil with good (Romans 12:14, 21).

Therefore, any person who continually justifies his sin before God is unworthy to partake of Communion. Rather than finding mercy and grace, he will find himself eating and drinking judgment upon himself.

The Communion of the bread and cup represents our covenant relationship with the Father through Jesus Christ. To walk in covenant requires a continual cleansing of our hearts from sin. It demands that we walk in an attitude of love toward all men. Wrong motives must be repented of if we want to partake of the blessings [including healing] of the bread and cup. This is what Paul meant when he wrote,

> But let a man examine himself, and so let him eat of the bread and drink of the cup (1 Corinthians 11:28)

If we are willing to judge ourselves, honestly examine our innermost motives and desires, and turn from sin, then the blood of Jesus will cleanse us from all unrighteousness and we will not be judged with the world (v. 31).

When discipline from the Lord is necessary (v. 32), He will correct us in such a way as to produce purity within our hearts. Our response must be one of true humility. We must choose to deal with everything He shows us that is contrary to His will. Then He will come and work within us, transforming us into His own like-ness, thereby removing every obstacle that would hinder our heal-ing.

**Practical Admonitions**. No study of the subject of healing would be complete without mentioning the fact that God has estab-lished certain natural laws concerning proper eating habits and rest, which, if not obeyed, can result in sickness. We must realize that believing in healing is not an alternative to obeying the laws of health. Proper care of the body is very closely associated with good health.

Many Christians appear to ignore this fact entirely; yet, they still want to believe for the healing of their bodies. Permanent health, however, will never occur as long as they're abusing their bodies. For example, overeating and excessive weight gain are the direct causes for some illnesses and a contributing factor in many others. The organs of the body, such as the heart, stomach and liver, become so overworked that it's impossible for them to carry out their normal functions. This results in heart and liver disease, diabetes, kidney trouble and many other ailments.

There are those who have requested prayer for healing who desperately need a change in their eating habits. If they ever received healing, it would probably be temporary because they would destroy their health through the same behavior which probably attributed to their sickness in the first place.

The Bible says we are to be temperate in all things (1 Corinthians 9:25). **We are to eat to live and not live to eat.** God would remind each of us personally that,

> *...whether you eat or drink, or whatever you do, do all to the glory of God (1 Corinthians 10:31).*

A lack of proper rest is another major concern in the matter of healing. Under the older covenant it was commanded that the people of God should take one day in seven to rest. Why would God give such a command? One reason was to give the people a day to recover physically from all of their work. The human body is made in such a way that it not only needs a day of rest but also proper sleep every night.

Some believers harm their bodies under the mistaken idea that because time is so short and Christ is about to return, they dare not take any time for rest. During His earthly ministry, Jesus not only took time for rest but He instructed His disciples to do the same (Mark 6:31). Likewise, we should not push ourselves beyond our own strength and ability.

God's people need some real common sense in all of these matters! We can't expect to enjoy continuous health unless we are wise in the conduct of our everyday lives. It is an awesome thing to realize that our bodies are now the temple of the Holy Spirit (1 Corinthians 6:19-20) and to sin against our bodies in any way is to sin against the Lord. Let's begin to glorify God in our bodies which belong to Him.

At this point some of us may feel there are so many issues to deal with that healing may be too difficult to receive. In reality, nothing could be easier, provided we desire to be right with the Lord. The difficulties we face are often those we make for ourselves—either in our lack of simple faith or the desire to examine truth in the light of our own reason, rather than accepting it as the Word of God.

If there are still those of you who don't understand why a loved one or acquaintance failed to receive healing, allow God's Word to comfort your hearts:

> *The secret things belong to the Lord our God,* ***but those things which are revealed belong to us and to our children forever,*** *that we may do all the words of this law (Deuteronomy 29:29, emphasis added).*

We have seen through our study of the Word of God that Christ took our infirmities and bore our sicknesses (Matthew

8:17). God has also answered "yes" to every promise in His Word (2 Corinthians 1:20). These truths belong to us and we now have the privilege of believing them.

Let's be careful to base our faith on the Word of God alone and not on anyone's experience. Since God has said "yes" to our healing, we must not be satisfied with anything less than His will for our lives. As we have examined our hearts and have sought to obey His Word, let's begin to expect God to do what He said He would do!

# CHAPTER IV

# How to Receive Your Healing

## Divine Revelation

**A**s we begin this chapter, we need to understand that while we'll be studying certain key principles necessary for receiving healing, we can never view healing as something that will automatically come to us as the result of some "formula." Healing, instead, must be seen as a way of life–that which is birthed out of a growing, intimate relationship with the Healer [See my book entitled *ENJOYING GOD*, published by Relevant Books]. It's in our communion with Christ through prayer and meditation of the Word that we come to experience a deeper sense of His presence, as well as a greater revelation of both His character and His will.

**A Divine Revelation of God's Character**. Our knowledge of the character of God is the very foundation of our faith. All true faith begins here! We can't trust someone we don't know in an intimate way. The Psalmist said,

*And those who know Your name will put their trust*

*in You...(Psalm 9:10).*

It's as we know His Name [His character] through an ever-deepening relationship with Him that we can grow in our trust. Hebrews 11:6 tells us that "...He [God] is a rewarder of those who diligently seek Him." Many Christians go unrewarded because they simply seek the reward instead of seeking the Lord. They seek His hand [His blessings] without seeking His face [His presence].

In a very true sense, every call from God is a call to God. For example, the call to believe God for healing is first and foremost a call to an intimate relationship with the Healer. All of the promises He has made to us are really the means He uses to draw us closer to Himself (2 Peter 1:4).

**A Divine Revelation of God's Will**. It's also vital for us to understand that faith only operates within the framework of the will of God. In other words, there can be no real release of faith without a knowledge of God's will.

> *Now this is the confidence that we have in Him, that if we ask any thing according to His will, he hears us: And if we know that He hears us, whatever we ask, we know that we have the petitions that we have asked of Him (1 John 5:14-15).*

Therefore, in order for us to experience healing, we must be convinced from the Word that it's the will of God for us to be healed. We must be so convinced that healing is a part of the Gospel and the redemption of Christ, that even the best arguments of men opposing this truth will be unable to sway us. When we know for certain it's the will of God for us to be healed, it won't be difficult to believe He will do what we're sure He wants to do.

## A Clean Heart

Another key for receiving healing is to make sure our hearts are continually right before the Lord. We need to remember that healing is a walk of covenant with God. To those who "walk uprightly" it is said, "...no good thing will He withhold..." (Psalm 84:11).

Being in covenant with the Lord means that, from our side, everything we are and have belongs to Him. We're His Bride! Because we've been bought with a price, it's only right that we give ourselves completely to Him (1 Corinthians 6:20). As we yield our bodies to the Lord, God promises to be "...**the Lord for the body**" (1 Corinthians 6:13, emphasis added).

If we're willing to love Christ with all of our hearts and allow Him to be Lord over every part of our lives, then Christ will be our covenant Healer.

## Faith

After we're convinced that healing is the will of God and our hearts have been cleansed by the washing of the Word, the next step is to appropriate by faith what God has already provided through His Son, Jesus Christ.

When God led the children of Israel out of Egypt, He had a further blessing in store for them. He not only promised to bring them **out** from the bondage of Pharaoh, but He also pledged to bring them **into** a new land.

When the Israelites finally crossed the Jordan River and entered Canaan, God said,

*Every place that the sole of your foot will tread*

*upon I **have** given you, as I said to Moses (Joshua 1:3, emphasis added).*

From God's perspective, He had already given them the land. Every step they took was on conquered ground, but they had to claim and possess it before it actually became theirs.

We, as believers today, also walk on conquered territory. Sickness has been overcome by the blood of Jesus. Healing belongs to us as a part of the new covenant; God has provided it for us. Yet, we still have to appropriate and possess our healing by faith before it will actually be ours.

Some people have said, "If God wants me to be healed, He'll just have to give it to me. He knows all my needs. If He doesn't heal me, then I guess He just doesn't want me to be healed." We must see, however, that God has already done all He's going to do about our healing. Our heavenly Father gave us healing as part of our inheritance in Christ nearly two thousand years ago, and He's waiting for us to take by faith what legally belongs to us!

Immediately before Jesus' death, when He said, "It is finished," He meant that the work of redemption was finished–completed in God's eyes. (See John 19:30.) As far as He is concerned, we were healed when Jesus bore the wounds in His body on the Cross. This same idea is reiterated in Matthew 8:17:

*He Himself took [past tense] our infirmities, and bore [past tense] our sicknesses.*

It's further reinforced through Peter who said,

*Who Himself bore our sins in His own body on the tree, that we, having died to sins, might live for right-*

*eousness–by whose stripes you **were** healed (1 Peter 2:24, emphasis added).*

Although the promises of God have legally been made ours, they don't come to us automatically. We must take by faith what He's already provided.

Just as we experienced our new birth by a definite act of faith, all of God's other promises must be received by a similar act of faith. It's true that God knows all of our needs even before we pray. Yet, we will receive only what we specifically ask for in faith (Matthew 7:7-11; James 4:2).

What does it mean to "ask in faith"? Jesus gives us a clue in Mark 11:24, when He says,

> *...Whatever things you ask when you pray, believe that you receive them, and you will have them.*

In this verse Christ clearly explains how to pray the prayer of faith. In childlike faith we're to make our requests to the Father in Jesus' Name, simply believing we receive the answers to our prayers the moment we ask. Notice, we're to believe we receive when we pray, not when the circumstances seem to improve.

While it may be difficult for us to believe we're healed until we see or feel some change, Mark 11:24 doesn't read: "Whatever things you ask for, when you see or feel them, then believe you've received them." The Word of God doesn't teach that seeing is believing; it teaches, instead, that believing is seeing. David said,

> *I would have lost heart, unless I had believed That I would see the goodness of the LORD In the land of the living (Psalm 27:13).*

When Martha's faith wavered at the tomb of Lazarus, Jesus said to her,

> *...Did I not say to you that if you would believe you would see the glory of God (John 11:40)?*

Also, the woman with the issue of blood first believed, and then felt in her body that she was healed (Mark 5:25-34).

Faith, then feeling, is the order for healing from which the Father never departs. When we pray for healing, or any other promise for that matter, Christ authorizes us to consider our prayer answered the moment we pray.

Faith believes God has already done what we have asked Him to do. We are to believe it is done, not because we see it done, but because God's Word declares it done. When God's Word is the only basis for believing our prayer is answered, we can have the assurance that our faith is strong.

God will not begin to manifest our healing until after we believe He has heard our prayer (1 John 5:14-15). The manifestation always comes after we believe. It may come a moment after we pray; then again, it may take a week, a month, or even longer before the answer is visible. Yet, if we expect to see the answer, we must receive it by faith even before we see it manifested.

Many of us often continue praying again and again for the same thing, hoping God will be moved by our repetition. However, God is not moved by repetition (Matthew 6:7); He is only moved by faith. This concept may be hard for some of us to embrace, especially the way we've come to understand the parable of the widow and the unjust judge (Luke 18:1-8). We know, however, that the truth Jesus was setting forth in the story would never contradict what He had already taught on other occasions. In teaching this parable, Jesus was simply explaining the importance of **persistence** in prayer.

For example, when we claim healing from the Lord and have to wait for its manifestation, we're to demonstrate persistence by reminding God of His promise. God loves to see His children believing His Word so strongly that they're willing to stand on it in spite of contrary circumstances. It was persistence that moved the heart of the unjust judge. How much more will persistent faith move the heart of our loving heavenly Father!

For five years a woman had prayed for the healing of her glaucoma. One evening when she heard me teach from Mark 11:24, she decided to pray for her healing one last time and simply believe the Lord. She asked Jesus to heal her, and thanked Him for the finished work. She then surrounded herself with the promises of God, fully expecting the manifestation at any time. For six weeks, however, there was no improvement in her physical condition. Nevertheless, she persistently stood on the Word of God, and later told of the wonderful manifestation of her healing, having been completely set free from glaucoma.

Many fail to receive healing because they believe what their five physical senses tell them instead of what the Word of God declares. Through faith in God's Word, we learn not to look at the circumstances. We can only know God and understand His Word through faith. The Bible says that

> ...*without faith it is **impossible** to please Him, for he who comes to God must believe that He is, and that He is a rewarder of those who diligently seek Him (Hebrews 11:6, emphasis added).*

It's also clear from 2 Corinthians 5:7 that we're to walk by faith and not by sight because the things of God can't be discerned and appropriated by the five senses.

What is faith? The biblical definition of faith is found in Hebrews 11:1.

*Now faith is the substance [reality] of things hoped for, the evidence of things not seen.*

Faith is a reality and stands in the place of the answer to our prayer until the answer is manifested in the visible realm. This means that when we claim our healing by faith, our faith takes the place of our healing until it's manifested. Our faith is as real to God as the healing will be to us when we see it manifested.

For example, if the reflection of an object can be seen in a mirror, then the object itself exists in reality. Our faith is the exact image of that for which we ask. Since an image is but the reflection of reality, when faith is present in our hearts, it means that the things for which we've asked are real in the spiritual realm. All we need to do is wait for the manifestations.

According to Hebrews 11:1, faith is also the evidence or proof that we have what we've prayed for before we see it. If we could see the answer with the natural eye, no faith would be required, because faith is the evidence of things **not seen**. When we believe in our hearts that we have our healing before we see it manifested (Mark 11:24), our faith proves we have that for which we prayed.

Notice also that Hebrews 11:1 begins with the phrase, "Now faith is." Faith is always **now** [present tense]. Hope projects everything into the future, but faith receives the answer as soon as it prays! While hope says, "I'm going to get it," faith declares, "I now have it."

Those who feel God will heal them someday may never experience healing because God has not promised to heal anyone "someday." He has already stated in His Word that we were legally healed when Jesus died on the Cross.

We need to accept our healing the moment we pray, believing that we are healed even before the circumstances change. Since our faith is the actual proof or evidence that we have our healing, we can be sure that the healing we desire of the Lord will be manifested.

The Bible teaches that an individual is to believe he's saved and confess his salvation on the basis of God's promise alone, even before he may feel the joy of sins forgiven. The joy and the feelings will eventually come if he will only believe and accept the gift of salvation by faith.

In the very same way, the sick must believe they are healed, regardless of how they feel; they must believe they are well on the basis of God's Word alone. As they are willing to stand firm on the Word of God, believing it's done, the joy of healing will be experienced!

We are not advocating "mind over matter" techniques as some might suspect. Neither are we denying the reality of sickness and pain as do the promoters of Christian Science philosophy. Sickness and pain are definitely real! The Bible doesn't try to hide the fact that Christians can get sick. However, when we appropriate any of the promises of God by faith, we are encouraged in Scripture not to look at our circumstances but, instead, to fix our attention on Christ.

Remember, the waves were just as high when Peter walked on the water as they were when he began to sink. As long as he didn't consider the circumstances, they couldn't hinder him; but the moment he took his eyes off Christ and centered his attention on the wind and the waves, he began to sink. If we become occupied with our circumstances and feelings, instead of His Word, we will lose what God has offered to us. On the other hand, by steadfastly looking beyond our problems to what our heavenly Father has said, we will partake of all that He has promised to us.

Many individuals begin to experience the manifestation of their healing and then lose it because they turn their attention from the Word of God to their circumstances and feelings. After taking the step of faith for healing, we must determine to keep our attention on Christ and His Word. The Bible says,

> *My son, give attention to my words; Incline your ear to my sayings. Do not let them depart from your eyes; Keep them in the midst of your heart; For they are life to those who find them, and health [Hebrew: medicine] to all their flesh (Proverbs 4:20-22).*

Here we're instructed to keep ourselves occupied with God's Word alone. If we do, there won't be room for doubt, fear, and discouragement.

Probably one of the greatest lessons on faith we could ever study is the example of Abraham,

> *who, contrary to hope, in hope believed, so that he became the father of many nations, according to what was spoken, "So shall your descendants be." And not being weak in faith, he did not consider his own body, already dead,(since he was about a hundred years*

118

*old), and the deadness of Sarah's womb. He did not waver at the promise of God through unbelief, but was strengthened in faith, giving glory to God, and being fully convinced that what He had promised He was also able to perform (Romans 4:18-21).*

Abraham didn't consider the evidence of his physical senses which testified that he was almost one hundred years old, far too old to become the father of children. He was also fully aware of the barrenness of his wife Sarah. According to nature, the birth of Isaac was impossible. Nevertheless, Abraham believed God and, by continuing to remember God's promise, experienced the miracle.

If we're continually occupied with our problems, instead of the Word of God, we will end up questioning the faithfulness of God. It says in the Book of Jonah, "They that observe lying vanities forsake their own mercy" (Jonah 2:8, KJV). Our heavenly Father never refuses to bestow mercy upon His children, but many Christians "forsake" His mercy by always being occupied with their circumstances.

We can't allow our physical senses to rule us if we're to live by faith. We may accept the evidence of our senses as long as it doesn't contradict the Word of God; however, when our five senses tell us one thing but the Scriptures reveal another, we **must** believe the Scriptures.

Keep in mind that faith is the evidence of things not seen. We may not see the answer to our prayers or feel any better after praying for our healing. So how do we know God has answered our prayers? Faith in our hearts is the only proof we need. We believe the things we have claimed exist because God's Word says they do. Our faith doesn't rest on any physical evidence but on biblical revelation. We choose to believe the promises of One who can't lie (Numbers 23:19-20; Romans 3:4).

Faith may appear to be irrational to many, but it's actually the most rational thing in the universe. Faith sees God's promises and His faithfulness as more certain than the foundations of the world. It refuses to be limited by the boundaries of logic or reason.

When the twelve spies came back from their exploration of Canaan, ten of them said that the land was inhabited with giants and that it wasn't reasonable to think that they could conquer them. Their conclusion was perfectly logical. However, two of the spies, Joshua and Caleb, held to the promise of God and believed the land could be taken from their enemies. They didn't the existence of the giants, but neither did they overlook the faithfulness of the God who had promised them victory in their battles.

The ten spies went as far as their reason could carry them; Joshua and Caleb went as far as logic would take them and then allowed faith to carry them the rest of the way. Faith always goes beyond reason and enables us to reach into the invisible realm and lay hold of "things hoped for" and "things not seen."

## Confession

Another vital principle necessary for obtaining healing from Christ is that of confession. While the message of confession over the last few years has been misapplied and in some cases abused, in Scripture there is a definite connection between believing and speaking.

This link between faith and confession is clearly seen in Mark 11:23, where Jesus said,

*...whoever says to this mountain, 'Be removed and be cast into the sea,' and does not doubt in his heart, but believes that those things he **says** will be done, he will have whatever he **says** (emphasis added).*

Notice, Jesus did not say one receives just by believing, but He said that a man "will have whatever he says."

Again, in Matthew 17:20, Jesus said,

*...If you have faith as a mustard seed, you will **say** to this mountain, 'Move from here to there,' and it will move; and nothing will be impossible for you (emphasis added).*

Neither of these verses can be limited to prayer alone. The words to which Jesus referred were not words expressed through prayer. When someone prays, he speaks to God; yet, here the disciples were instructed to speak to a mountain.

These two passages, instead, reveal the awesome power of faith when translated into words. According to Christ, believing with the heart that the mountain will move is not enough. What's in the heart must be expressed with the mouth. It's what the Apostle Paul had reference to when he said in 2 Corinthians 4:13, "...we also believe, and therefore speak."

Faith and confession are two sides of the same coin. It's the confession of our mouths that releases the faith in our hearts. This truth is further communicated by Paul in Romans 10:9-10:

*...if you confess with your mouth the Lord Jesus and believe in your heart that God has raised Him from the dead, you will be saved. For with the heart one*

*believes unto righteousness, and with the mouth confession is made unto salvation.*

According to the Word of God, salvation doesn't occur until after a confession of faith is made. Faith in the heart must inevitably be confessed with the mouth. The Greek word "confess" literally means "to agree with" or "to speak the same language." Confession is simply saying the same thing God has said about His promises, affirming our faith in His Word.

Therefore, if we expect to receive our healing, we must confess with the Scriptures that we are healed (Isaiah 53:5; 1 Peter 2:24). While we are not advocating mere "lip service" or just a repetition of words, if we really believe in our hearts that we are healed, it will be expressed by what we say or confess.

This is confirmed even more by Jesus' words in Matthew 12:34,

*...For out of the abundance of the heart the mouth speaks.*

The mouth reveals not only what's in the heart but also what dominates the heart. When we speak, we lift the curtain off of our hearts and uncover its contents.

When David chose to do battle with Goliath, he said to Saul,

*...The LORD, who delivered me from the paw of the lion and from the paw of the bear, He will deliver me from the hand of this Philistine....(1 Samuel 17:37).*

This was his confession of faith. Armed with nothing more than five stones, David marched toward the giant, declaring,

*This day the LORD will deliver you into my hand,*

*and I will strike you and take your head from you. And this day I will give the carcasses of the camp of the Philistines to the birds of the air and the wild beasts of the earth, that all the earth may know that there is a God in Israel (v. 46).*

While the army of Israel was filled with fear, David was filled with faith. Because God had delivered him from harm so many times before, he believed God would do it again and, therefore, confessed the victory even in advance.

In contrast, the children of Israel had so much doubt concerning God's ability to bring them into the land of Canaan, they continually complained that they would perish in the wilderness. (Read Numbers 13-14.) Because they believed and confessed they would die before obtaining their inheritance, God said,

*...As I live...just as you have **spoken** in My hearing, so I will do to you: The carcasses of you who have complained against Me shall fall in this wilderness, all of you who were numbered, according to your entire number, from twenty years old and above. Except for Caleb the son of Jephunneh and Joshua the son of Nun, you shall by no means enter the land which I swore I would make you dwell in (Numbers 14:28-30, emphasis added).*

From these two different examples we can see that what we believe and confess is of the utmost importance. When our confession agrees with the Word of God, we will receive what He has promised. If our confession doesn't harmonize with what the Scriptures say, the promises will be negated in our lives.

Some may ask at this point, "But wouldn't it be a lie to confess the promises of God if, even after prayer, the circumstances haven't improved?" When we confess what God says about our situation, we can be sure we're speaking the truth. Remember, Romans 4:17 tells us that God

> *...calls those things which do not exist as though they did.*

When God came to Abram and promised his a son, He changed his name to Abraham, which in Hebrew means "father of a great multitude." For twenty-five years before the birth of Isaac, Abraham had to bear the stigma of what that name meant. To those around him, he must've appeared utterly foolish by using his new name. Yet, was Abraham lying by taking the name God had given him, even though it was years before he saw the fulfillment of the promise?

If God's Word says we're healed, we would be foolish to confess otherwise. To confess healing even in the face of adverse circumstances is simply an act of obedience to God's admonition to believe He has heard and answered our prayer (Mark 11:23-24; 1 John 5:14-15). Speaking the Word of God, especially in time of difficulty, glorifies the Lord. What could please Him more than hearing His people boldly voicing their faith in their heavenly Father in the midst of seemingly adverse circumstances?

Some years ago, a woman attended a meeting where I was speaking on the subject of faith. She was dying of cancer and had been told that she only had six months to live. After the message was over, she came forward for prayer. Although there was no apparent change in her condition, she left the meeting believing and confessing that the Lord had touched her. When she returned to her doctor for further examination, he could find no trace of cancer.

Hebrews 3:1 informs us that Jesus is the High Priest of our profession [Greek: confession]. As our High Priest, He continuously represents us before the Father. Whenever we confess the promises of God, Jesus takes our confession to the Father as evidence of our faith in His Word. On the basis of His intercession (Hebrews 7:25) and our faith in the finished work of the Cross, we're able to triumph over the enemy in every area of our lives.

Revelation 12:11 also tells us that we overcome Satan by the blood of the Lamb and the word of our testimony. When we appeal to the blood of Jesus and what it represents, as well as hold fast to the testimony of God's Word, we can have the assurance of the utter defeat of all the works of darkness. It's worth noting at this point that Christ always rebuked the devil and his works with the spoken word. He cast out demons and healed the sick, not by thoughts but by words, demonstrating the will of His Father.

From the example of Christ, we must learn to do the same. Whenever we find ourselves under any kind of attack, whether spiritual or physical, we must speak the Word of God against it. It's the power of God's Word, not our words, that overcomes all the power of the enemy.

Therefore, if sickness strikes us, there are three factors to consider if we expect to receive the manifestation of our healing:

1. What God says about our sicknesses (Psalm 103:3; Isaiah 53:5)

2. What Satan says about our condition ("You're not well; the symptoms are getting worse and you just might die.")

3. What we believe and say about our condition

If we're convinced that healing is the will of our Father, then we must speak words that harmonize with His will. What we believe and confess will determine the outcome, for we have the choice of agreeing either with Satan or with God.

## Acting Faith

For faith to be effective, our actions must correspond with what we say we believe. The Scriptures teach that when true faith is present it will automatically produce corresponding actions of faith. James says,

> *What does it profit, my brethren, if someone says he has faith but does not have works? Can faith save him? If a brother or sister is naked and destitute of daily food, and one of you says to them, "Depart in peace, be warmed and filled," but you do not give them the things that are needed for the body, what does it profit? Thus also faith by itself, if it does not have works, is dead. But someone will say, "You have faith, and I have works." Show me your faith without your works, and I will show you my faith by my works (James 2:14-18).*

When four men came to Jesus bearing a palsied man (Mark 2:1-12), the Bible tells us that He saw their faith. Obviously, faith can't be seen because it's not a visible substance. What Jesus actually saw was their faith at work as the men took the roof apart to get the sick man to Him. When Jesus said to the palsied man, "...arise, take up your bed, and go to your house," the man believed the spoken word of Jesus and acted upon it (v. 11). His actions

126

proved his faith, for verse 12 says, "Immediately he arose, took up the bed, and went out in the presence of them all...."

True faith is always active. Throughout the Bible, men and women of faith were men and women of action. Those who believed God's Word were those who acted on the Word. Read, for example, the account of the faith of the saints in Hebrews 11. The writer describes their faith by speaking about their works. In other words, they did something to demonstrate their faith.

Many Christians confess that they believe the Word of God is true; yet, at the same time, they act as though they don't believe. Often people are willing to talk about their "faith" but are hesitant to act on the Word of God. Faith, however, is acting on the revealed will of God.

To believe God is to obey Him. In Hebrews 11:19, we are told Abraham believed that, if necessary, God would raise Isaac from the dead. What was the corresponding action that accompanied his faith? He made plans to sacrifice his son as God had commanded.

In Luke 17, we read of ten lepers who saw Jesus and cried out, "...Jesus, Master, have mercy on us" (v. 13)! We're told that "...when he saw them, He said to them, Go, show yourselves to the priests..." (v. 14). This was quite significant, for when a leper was healed the law required that he be given a clean bill of health by the priests before he could be allowed back into society as a normal citizen.

From all outward appearance, these lepers weren't healed. They were still bearing the evidence of the disease in their bodies when Jesus commanded them to go and show themselves to the priests. We can't imagine the thoughts that must've crossed their minds–the priests would openly rebuke them, the people would mock them, and they would become a laughingstock in the community. It was bad enough being a leper without experiencing added pressures.

Nevertheless, the Bible says that "...as they went, they were cleansed" (v. 14). When were these lepers healed? They were healed as they acted on the command of Christ. Had they waited until their healings were manifested before going to the priests, they would have remained lepers.

When God told Joshua He would part the waters of the Jordan River so the whole nation of Israel could cross over on dry ground, the Scriptures tell us that it was not until

> ...the feet of the priests who bore the ark dipped in the edge of the water...that the waters which came down from upstream stood still, and rose in a heap...and all Israel crossed over on dry ground, until all the people had crossed completely over the Jordan (Joshua 3:15-17).

Notice, the waters parted when the priests stepped forward in obedience to God's command.

Are you facing some insurmountable problem in spite of all your praying and believing? Examine your obedience and response to God's Word. Have you done all that God has instructed you to do about the particular matter, or have you been waiting for the "parting of the waters" before you put your next foot forward?

Many are willing to act on the word of their doctor, knowing that even though they still appear to be sick, they will eventually recover. How much more should we act upon the Word of our covenant Physician when He says, "...I am the LORD who heals you" (Exodus 15:26).

Although we can't tell people how to act their faith and we can't lay down any hard and fast rules concerning the exercise of faith, we do know that if they really believe God has heard and answered their prayer, they'll act accordingly.

When a healing isn't manifested immediately, the Lord will always show us what to do to demonstrate our faith. There were those under the ministry of Jesus who weren't healed instantly; nevertheless, Christ gave them clear instructions regarding what to do to put their faith into action. The blind man in John 9:7 had his eyes anointed with clay and was then told by Jesus to go wash in the pool of Siloam. As he obeyed Jesus' words, he received his eyesight. Again, the ten lepers were challenged to go show themselves to the priests. In each case, these individuals did what Jesus told them to do. They were relying upon the words of Christ and believing the healing was theirs before it was ever manifested.

If we believe we're healed according to the Word of God, one of the primary things we'll do is thank the Lord for our healing. We read in Romans 4:20 that Abraham gave "glory to God" for the fulfillment of God's promise to him, long before the answer [Isaac] was manifested. While the walls of Jericho were still erect and standing, Joshua and the children of Israel shouted praises to God for delivering the city into their hands (Joshua 6). Because they believed God's promise, they acted their faith by marching around the city in obedience to God. As they marched and offered praise to the Lord, the walls fell and the victory became theirs.

Acting our faith by praising God in advance has always been one way the Lord has chosen for us to appropriate His promises.

Hebrews 13:15 instructs us that our "sacrifice of praise" is to be offered in advance for the blessings He has promised. Instead of listening to Satan, the father of lies, we must force him to listen to us as we praise God for His faithfulness regarding His covenant.

Real faith always rejoices in the promise of God as if it had already experienced the answer and was enjoying it. We should be so convinced that God's promises are true that we'll be willing to thank Him for their fulfillment and act upon them even before we see them manifested.

Since Christ "took our infirmities, and bore our sicknesses," let's begin praising Him for that. Instead of complaining about our aches and pains, let's rise up and take God at His Word, allowing Him to make His promises good in our lives. The more we act on God's Word, the stronger our faith will become.

We may apply all of the other principles found in this chapter, but if we don't act upon His promises when we pray, our faith will profit us nothing. Although we may not know the exact time when the manifestation will occur, it will come as we're acting in agreement with the Word of God. Therefore, let's be "...doers of the word, and not hearers only..." (James 1:22).

## Enduring Faith

One of the most important discoveries we will ever make in our walk of faith is that our heavenly Father doesn't operate according to our timetable. Although we should expect immediate manifestations of the answers to our prayers, sometimes there's a waiting period between the time we ask for something and the time we receive the manifestation. And for us as Christians, this can present some real problems.

We can find ourselves becoming impatient and frustrated with every passing day, while at the same time the enemy is whispering in our ears, "Has God said?" Satan would even have us believe that delay means denial.

The delays, however, are as much a part of God's overall purpose as are the manifestations of the promises themselves. Timing is always more important to the Lord than time. Whatever the reason is for the delay, we can take comfort in knowing that His ways are always perfect and that the delays are an integral part of His plan for our lives. Although we may not understand all the reasons for the delays, there are some things of which we can be certain.

First of all, God sometimes withholds the blessing until the blessing becomes of secondary importance. It's so easy to focus all our attention on the blessings rather than on the One who gives them. Only when our relationship with the Lord overshadows the blessing are we indeed ready to receive it. Hebrews 11:6 tells us that God is a rewarder of those who seek Him, not just the blessing.

Secondly, God uses the delays to mature our faith. Faith must be tested! An untried faith is an undependable faith. If there's a flaw in our faith, we need to know in order for it to be corrected. If we want a faith that will be equal to all the attacks ever thrown against it, we have to understand that the Father will allow our faith to be challenged in order that it may be strengthened. This is why James admonishes the Christian to

> ...count it all joy when you fall into various trials, knowing that the testing of your faith produces patience [Greek: endurance]. But let patience

*[endurance] have its perfect work, that you may be perfect [mature] and complete, lacking nothing (James 1:2-4).*

However, trials in themselves don't mature us; it is what we do during our trials that make the difference. If, for example, we become discouraged when our healing isn't manifested as quickly as we had hoped, our faith will become weak and frail. Yet, if we overcome in the trial by standing on the Word of God, we will not only experience the manifestation of our healing, but we will also grow in faith.

Thirdly, there can be delays in the manifestation of the answers to our prayers because Satan will try to contest everything we embrace by faith. During wartime, whenever soldiers make an advance against their enemies, they usually end up having to "dig in" under fire. When we, as Christians, strive to advance in faith, we're also challenging our enemy. If we aren't prepared for the battle, Satan will keep us from coming into what rightfully belongs to us.

When we appropriate the promises of God by faith, we must determine that we won't turn loose of the Word of God, in spite of all evidence to the contrary. As we hold fast to the precious promises and endure by faith, God will actually give us the **privilege** of weakening the enemy and ultimately overcoming him.

If we're going to see the fulfillment of any of God's promises, we must view faith as both an initial act and a continuous attitude. Faith will not only bring us to Christ with our need but will also keep us there if the need isn't immediately met. Of all the various facets of faith, this latter one is probably the most important. When the things for which we're believing seem impossible and beyond our reach, it's "enduring faith" that will keep us on course and our eyes fixed on the unchanging promises of God.

How can we endure until the promise is fulfilled and, at the same time, stand against the assaults of doubt and fear? First of all, if we've prayed for our healing and the symptoms haven't yet disappeared, we need to cease being anxious and fretful about the condition of our bodies. If we've committed our bodies to the Lord, we can be at peace, knowing that He'll take responsibility for every case entrusted to Him. How much better it is to be in communion with the Father, rejoicing in His faithfulness, and doing His will, than to be continually occupied with the problem!

Secondly, we must remind ourselves of God's faithfulness to us in times past. Remembering His goodness toward us from previous experiences is a great defense against discouragement and doubt. Moses, shortly before his death, rehearsed with the people all that God had done for them, admonishing them to **remember**. Israel, when confronted time and again with apparent disaster, believed her way to victory by recalling God's past mercies. The Psalmist declared,

> *I will remember the works of the LORD; Surely I will remember Your wonders of old. I will also meditate on all Your work, and talk of Your deeds (Psalm 77:11-12).*

How many times have we been delivered from difficulty by God's grace, only to find ourselves later facing another seemingly impossible situation and complaining because we feel God has abandoned us? **Forgetfulness is definitely hazardous to our health!**

In the third place, we must be careful to guard our faith, for Satan will try to trick us into thinking and talking about our problems instead of the Word of God. We are told in Hebrews 10:23 to

*...hold fast the confession of our hope without wavering, for He who promised is faithful.*

**We must maintain a continual confession of what we believe if we're to see the fulfillment of the promise.**

Many have claimed their healing by faith; however, when the healing wasn't manifested immediately or soon thereafter, they began to waver and doubt, giving up their confession of faith. As a result, they never experienced the manifestation of their healing.

Yet, how many will go to the doctor and faithfully follow his instructions, regardless of the time it takes for them to get well. They'll confess what the doctor says even if the symptoms don't improve or if they feel worse for a period of time.

How much more should we faithfully follow the instructions of the Great Physician, no matter how long it takes for our healing to manifest. We should be willing to confess what He says about our condition even if, for a while, we don't feel any better.

Fourthly, we need to realize that while waiting for the fulfillment of the promise, enduring faith will continue to pursue God's **present** will. This is clearly illustrated in Hebrews 10:35-36 where we read,

*Therefore do not away your confidence, which has great reward. For you have need of endurance, so that after you have done the will of God, you may receive the promise.*

Receiving what God has promised requires obedience. We can't expect God to keep His promise if we're not willing to do His will.

During periods of testing, Satan's strategy is to disrupt us from doing the will of God by trying to fill us with fear and uncertainty. Many of us have known what it's like to be so preoccupied with some problem that our hearts were depleted of confidence in the Word of God. Most of us have experienced the complacency that comes with discouragement.

To take the initiative away from the devil, we must literally do what is said in Psalm 37:3:

*Trust in the Lord, **and do good**...(emphasis added).*

Having committed the situation to the Father, we're to focus our attention on everyday obedience. Doing good is evidence that we're trusting in the Lord. If the trial we're going through upsets us so much that it prevents us from seeking only the Kingdom of God and His righteousness, then we haven't fully committed the matter to the Lord.

Finally, we must understand that enduring faith is always accompanied by **anticipation**. True endurance isn't waiting with resignation but, instead, waiting with expectation. While few things in life are as unappealing as waiting, it's the attitude of anticipation that makes endurance possible.

Endurance is never passive. The "spirit of faith" continuously radiates with hope as it looks forward to the manifestation of the promise!

The Psalmist tells us that waiting for the Lord is like waiting for the morning (Psalm 130:6). In waiting for the morning, we can always depend on two things: first of all, nothing we can do will hurry it; secondly, it will eventually come. Those who wait for the morning are never disappointed; neither are those who wait for the Lord.

Therefore, let nothing discourage you. Refuse to allow any symptom or circumstance to change your attitude toward the Word of God. Once and for all, settle it in your heart that both the will of God and the promises of God are going to be fulfilled in your life. Accept nothing less than the healing He has provided for you.[5]

---

5. There are several avenues we can take in receiving healing–the personal prayer of faith (Mark 11:22-24), the prayer of agreement (Matthew 18:19), the laying on of hands by another person (Mark 16:18), and the anointing of oil by the elders of the church (James 5:14-15)–but the principles of faith found within this chapter must still be applied if an individual is to walk in healing and health.

# CHAPTER V

# Keeping Your Healing

Years ago I was troubled because I couldn't understand why some people who had received healing later seemed to lose their healing and experience the return of their former symptoms. Some had said to me, "I felt perfectly fine for some time after prayer; then suddenly all the symptoms returned, and I haven't been feeling well ever since. What went wrong?"

Although it's not the will of God for an illness to return to a believer, we must remember that the devil is an active and intelligent adversary who gives no ground except what is forcibly taken from him by faith. Whenever Satan loses any ground, he is constantly looking for an opportunity to take it back again.

This principle of warfare is addressed by Jesus in Luke 11:24-26:

> *When an unclean spirit is goes out of a man, he goes through dry places, seeking rest; and finding none, he says, 'I will return to my house from which I came.' And when he comes, he finds it swept and put in order. Then he goes and takes with him seven other*

*spirits more wicked than himself, and they enter and dwell there; and the last state of that man is worse than the first.*

It is significant that Christ said this immediately after He had healed a man by casting out a spirit of dumbness. (See vs. 14-23.) While verses 24-26 are often interpreted in a spiritual sense, they actually refer to what can happen to individuals who have been healed but haven't continued to fill their hearts and minds with God's Word.

It's erroneous to believe that if a genuine healing is experienced, then it will automatically last without regard to faith or holiness. To the man who had been healed of a condition that had lasted for thirty-eight years, Jesus said,

*...See, you have been made well. Sin no more, lest a worse thing come upon you (John 5:14).*

When we have been released from "oppression" of any kind, whether it be from sin, demonic activity, or even sickness, it's imperative that our hearts and minds stay pure and grounded in the Word of God. We must never allow the enemy to find our "homes" empty, because there is the danger of a counter-attack. For this reason, we must continuously remain in faith by feeding on the Scriptures and abiding in intimate communion with the Father.

Satan, who is aware that faith is his enemy, is constantly seeking to destroy it. Whenever we feel any pain or see any symptoms which resemble our previous illness, Satan will immediately suggest that we were never healed or our healing wasn't complete because it did not seem to last. If the promises of God are not clear in our thinking, we may find it easier to believe the lies of the devil than the truths of God's Word. Doubt and fear will grip our hearts, and the adversary will try to take advantage of us by attempting to try to put the sickness back on us. If we believe what the symptoms seem to indicate rather than what Christ has already done for us, Satan will take from us the ground which we took by faith from him.

Therefore, if an illness seems to return, don't become frightened and discouraged. **Resist** the symptoms with the Word of God. Don't accept them. **Refuse** to sign for the "package" that Satan is trying to offer you. **Review** by faith your covenant benefits. You were healed! It was a part of the finished work of the Cross. Begin to praise God for your deliverance, and the symptoms will eventually succumb to the power of God.

If we're to keep our healing, it's also important for us to guard our hearts from the doubts of others. Continually listening to the skepticism and uncertainty of others can actually weaken our faith. Once we've committed our circumstances to the Lord, it's wise not to discuss what we've received by faith with those who don't believe. We need to be gracious and patient with people, but we can't allow their opinions to sway our faith.

As we've already seen, it's possible to lose a healing if we allow doubt to affect our faith. One man who was healed of a crippling disease lost his healing and was again confined to a wheelchair because he listened to the doubts of friends who didn't believe healing was for today.

In addition, seek an atmosphere of faith in which to fellowship. There are churches where the Gospel is preached, lives are transformed, and the sick are healed. Identify with those groups where you can find food for your faith and where your testimony can be given to encourage others.

God has promised you, as a believer, longevity of life (Psalm 91:14-16). Take to heart what the Lord has provided for you through His blood, and learn to walk in God's "*covenant of healing.*"

# Healing Scriptures

**For all the promises of God in Him are Yes, and in Him Amen, to the glory of God through us (2 Corinthians 1:20).**

If you diligently heed to the voice of the LORD your God and do what is right in His sight, give ear to his commandments and keep all His statutes, I will put none of the diseases on you which I have brought on the Egyptians. For I am the LORD who heals you (Exodus 15:26).

So you shall serve the LORD your God, and He will bless your bread and your water. And I will take sickness away from the midst of you (Exodus 23:25).

And the LORD will take away from you all sickness, and will afflict you with none of the terrible diseases of Egypt which you have known, but will lay them on all those who hate you (Deuteronomy 7:15).

And if you are Christ's, then you are Abraham's seed, and heirs according to the promise (Galatians 3:29).

...God anointed Jesus of Nazareth with the Holy Spirit and with power, who went about doing good and healing all who were oppressed by the devil, for God was with Him (Acts 10:38).

...For this purpose the Son of God was manifested, that He might destroy the works [e.g., sickness] of the devil (1 John 3:8).

The thief does not come except to steal, and to kill, and to destroy: I have come that they may have life, and that they may have it more abundantly (John 10:10).

And Jesus went about all Galilee,..healing all kinds of sickness and all kinds of disease among the peoplefsafs f.and they brought to Him all sick people who were afflicted with various diseases and torments, and those which were demon-possessed, and those which were epileptic, and paralytics; and He healed them (Matthew 4:23-24).

Jesus Christ is the same yesterday, today, and forever (Hebrews 13:8).

Who forgives all your iniquities, Who heals all your diseases (Psalm 103:3).

Surely he has borne our griefs [Hebrew: sicknesses] And carried our sorrows [Hebrew: pains]: Yet we esteemed Him stricken, smitten by God, and afflicted. But He was wounded for our transgressions, He was bruised for our iniquities; The chastisement of our peace was upon Him, And by His stripes we are healed (Isaiah 53:4-5).

When evening had come, they brought to Him many who were demon-possessed. And He cast out the spirits with a word, and healed all who were sick, that it might be fulfilled which was spoken by Isaiah the prophet, saying: "He Himself took our infirmities, And bore our sicknesses" (Matthew 8:16-17).

Christ has redeemed us from the curse of the law, having become a curse for us (for it is written, "Cursed is every one who hangs on a tree"). (Galatians 3:13; The curse of the law includes sickness. See Deuteronomy 28:15-61.)

Who Himself bore our sins in His own body on the tree, that we, having died to sins, might live for righteousness–by whose stripes you were healed (1 Peter 2:24).

He sent his word and healed them, And delivered them from their destructions (Psalm 107:20).

My son, give attention to my words; Incline your ear to my sayings. Do not let them depart from your eyes; Keep them in the midst of your heart; For they are life for those who find them, And health to all their flesh (Proverbs 4:20-22).

"And whatever you ask [e. g. , healing] in My name, that I will do, that the Father may be glorified in the Son. If you ask any thing in My name, I will do it" (John 14:13-14).

"For assuredly, I say to you, whoever says to this mountain [e.g., sickness and disease], 'Be removed and be cast into the sea,' and does not doubt in his heart, but believes that those things he says will be done, he will have whatever he says" (Mark 11:23).

"Therefore I say to you, Whatever things you ask [e.g., healing] when you pray, believe that you receive them, and you will have them" (Mark 11:24).

"And these signs will follow those who believe: In My name they will cast out demons; they will speak with new tongues; they shall take up serpents; and if they drink anything deadly, it will by no means hurt them; they will lay hands on the sick, and they will recover" (Mark 16:17-18).

But if the Spirit of Him who raised Jesus from the dead dwells in you, He who raised Christ from the dead will also give life to your mortal [physical] bodies through His Spirit who dwells in you (Romans 8:11).

Now the body is not for sexual immorality but for the Lord, **and the Lord for the body** (1 Corinthians 6:13, emphasis added).

Or do you not know that your **body** is the temple of the Holy Spirit who is in you, whom you have from God, and you are not your own? For you were bought [redeemed] at a price; therefore glorify God in your **body** and in your spirit, which are God's (1 Corinthians 6:19-20, emphasis added).

Is anyone among you sick? Let him call for the elders of the church, and let them pray over him, anointing him with oil in the name of the Lord. And the prayer of faith will save [heal] the sick, and the Lord will raise him up. And if he has committed sins, he will be forgiven (James 5:14-15).

Now this is the confidence that we have in Him, that if we ask any thing according to His will [e.g., healing], he hears us. And if we know that he hears us, whatever we ask, we know that we have the petitions that we asked of Him (1 John 5:14-15).

Beloved, I pray that you may prosper in all things and be in health, just as your soul prospers (3 John 2).

No evil shall befall you, Nor shall any **plague** come near your dwelling (Psalm 91:10, emphasis added) .

He shall call upon Me, and I will answer him; I will be with him in trouble; I will deliver him and honor him. With **long life** I will satisfy him, and show Him my salvation [the Hebrew implies healing] (Psalm 91:15-16, emphasis added).

144

# ENJOYING GOD

What greater way is there to glorify God in your life than by simply enjoying Him? It's simple, but it's radical. Some may even call it revolutionary. Yet it's the heartbeat of Christianity.

Enjoying God will challenge and encourage you to pursue a passionate, intimate relationship with God. The book exposes misunderstandings that can damage and jeopardize your faith, and it uncovers a biblical understanding of God as Father. Enjoying God will move you from duty to delight in your relationship with Christ.

---

"I loved this book. From the introduction there was a spirit of grace, of intimacy with God, that was ever wooing and drawing me closer to the Lord's heart. I felt, in a way, cleansed, not merely from sin but from serving God from duty rather than joy. This book goes beyond informing to liberating."
**Francis Frangipane**
**Author and Senior Minister of River of Life Church,**
**Cedar Rapids, Iowa**

---

"As much as I am committed to the Great Commission, I am more committed to the Great Commandment. I don't really believe you can fulfill the evangelistic mandate without being a great lover. Great lovers make great laborers in God's kingdom. S.J. Hill teaches you how to cultivate that love relationship with Jesus. I highly recommend this book."
**Che Ahn**
**President, The Call D.C. Senior Pastor of Harvest Rock Church,**
**Pasadena, California**

---

"Do you want to enjoy, experience and express more of God's presence? This book is your gift from God to enable you to discover and develop a whole new dimension of relationship with Jesus. This isn't hype. It's right here in your hands!"
**Larry Tomczak**
**Author and Pastor of Christ the King Church, Atlanta, Georgia**

## PERSONAL REVIVAL

How can we make our relationship with God the highest priority of our lives? How can we experience personal revival, and how can we sustain that life of passion, fire, and renewal?

In this important, clearly written book by S. J. Hill, you will find both inspiration as well as practical instruction. Drawing on a wide range of sources, and writing from years of personal experience, S. J. has put together a rich biblical study that will help every believer who is hungry for a deeper and closer walk with Jesus. It will provide meat for the mature and solid food for the serious, showing the way to maintain personal revival in the valley as well as on the mountain top. You will be stirred and helped as you read the pages of this book.

---

S.J. (Steve) Hill has captured the heart of the relationship of true brokenness and the power of anointing. This is a book from a real man of God speaking real things out of a real experience. That is what makes his insights so penetrating and life changing. When you read the book, you will not fear brokenness, you will desire it.

**Bob Phillips – Author and Bible teacher who co-pastored Times Square Church with David Wilkerson. He is currently the pastor of the Encourager Church in Houston, Texas.**

---

This book deals with the very crux of true revival – a broken and hungry heart before God. Don't allow its ease of reading to stop you from meditating upon these essential and biblical principles for *personal revival*. Read it, mark it, and read it again.

**David Ravenhill – Bible Teacher and Author of FOR GOD'S SAKE GROW UP! He is the son of the late Leonard Ravenhill.**

# About the Author

**S.J. Hill**

S. J. Hill is a gifted leader and teacher in the Body of Christ with over thirty years of experience in the ministry. He has pastored, as well as worked with David Hogan and Freedom Ministries in Mexico. S. J. has been on the faculty of the Brownsville Revival School of Ministry in Pensacola, Florida, and the F.I.R.E. School of Ministry. He has also worked with Mike Bickle at the International House of Prayer in Kansas City, Missouri, as well as taught at the Forerunner School of Ministry.

S. J. travels extensively throughout the world, teaching and calling believers to deep intimacy with God and radical commitment to Jesus Christ. His all-consuming passion is to see the Church come to an understanding of the beauty of God's personality.

S. J. has authored two other books – ENJOYING GOD and PERSONAL REVIVAL.

He and his wife, Pam, are the parents of two sons, Jonathan and Lance.

**To contact S. J. for speaking engagements, please email him at stevejhill@juno.com Check out his website at www.sjhill.com**